5-
m

Wildlife, Wild Death

Wildlife,

Rodger Yeager/Norman N. Miller

Wild Death

LAND USE AND SURVIVAL IN EASTERN AFRICA

State University of New York Press
in association with
The African-Caribbean Institute

SUNY Series in Environmental Public Policy
Lester W. Milbrath, Editor

PUBLISHED BY
STATE UNIVERSITY OF NEW YORK PRESS, ALBANY

© 1986 STATE UNIVERSITY OF NEW YORK

FOR INFORMATION, ADDRESS STATE UNIVERSITY OF NEW YORK PRESS,
STATE UNIVERSITY PLAZA, ALBANY, N.Y., 12246

LIBRARY OF CONGRESS CATALOGING IN PUBLICATION DATA

YEAGER, RODGER.
WILDLIFE, WILD DEATH.

BIBLIOGRAPHY: p. 162
INCLUDES INDEX.
1. WILDLIFE CONSERVATION—KENYA.   2. WILDLIFE
CONSERVATION—TANZANIA.   3. LAND USE—ENVIRONMENTAL
ASPECTS—KENYA.   4. LAND USE—ENVIRONMENTAL ASPECTS—
TANZANIA.   5. AGRICULTURAL ECOLOGY—KENYA.
6. AGRICULTURAL ECOLOGY—TANZANIA. I. MILLER, NORMAN N.,
1933-   II. TITLE.
QL84.6.K4Y43   1986   333.95′16′09676   86-5791
ISBN 0-88706-168-0
ISBN 0-88706-169-9 (pbk.)

10   9   8   7   6   5   4   3   2   1

To our families

Contents

Figures

Tables

Illustrations

Preface and Acknowledgements

As the final draft of this study nears completion, the agony of Africa fills the headlines. Food shortages, famine, and starvation threaten nineteen of the forty countries compressed into the tropical African mainland, countries containing nearly half the total African population. Crop-destroying and livestock-menacing drought touches most of the rest. In Europe and North America, public and private relief agencies struggle in a race against time to forestall mass annihilations in Chad, Ethiopia, and Mozambique, and also in Mali, Mauritania, Niger, and Sudan. A million or more people may die before the end of the next growing season, and the toll will be higher if the rains fail again.

Blame for this catastrophe is variously assigned to freakishly adverse weather conditions; to possibly more basic and permanent climatic changes; to unprecedented population growth that exceeds subsistence capacities; to an insensitive and even hostile international economic order; to internecine ethnic and religious violence; and last—but not least—to malevolent, corrupt, or merely inept ruling elites. Although each of these factors plays a part, no one or simple combination of them adequately explains how this world region, which until recently fed itself and exported food surpluses, could so quickly sink into a Malthusian horror of hunger and death that finds no parallel in modern times. This study suggests some of the underlying reasons for this tragedy, in the context of two countries where there is still time to act.

By the mid-1980s, Tanzania and Kenya were experiencing chronic droughts and grain shortages that necessitated more food aid imports than ever before. The general situation in which Africa finds itself and the trends clearly visible in Kenya and Tanzania have caused us to reorient our research interests in these societies. Originally limited to the political status of wildlife and wildlife refuges, we have expanded our agendas to include agricultural land use and environmental protection in the vicinities of these legally enfranchised sanctuaries. In Tanzania, in Kenya, and in other parts of eastern and southern Africa, the impending ecological disasters endanger not only human and livestock populations, but also many wild animal species unique to the continent which face the possibility of extinction.

Why, one might ask, amid all of this unfolding human misery, should we remain concerned with the creatures that inhabit eastern Africa's natural ecosystems? People need food, and food requires land. In countries like those we have studied, large tracts are set aside for wildlife. Because of their easily disturbed physical environments, these expanses are incapable of absorbing full-scale competition between agriculturalists and wild animals. If they are rendered uninhabitable, the Chadian, Ethiopian, and Mozambican calamities could spread southward and northward, indiscriminately claiming rural dwellers, livestock, game herds, and other wildlife species. Wildlife have much to contribute, not only to mankind in general, but also to the future development of the countries hosting them. Their loss would strike a serious blow to both sets of interests. In the most immediate sense, either humans and wild animals will coexist and prosper together, or they may perish together. Solutions to the problems of one group turn invariably on solutions to the problems of the other.

Because of their great magnitude and highly controversial nature, these issues can only be resolved through public policy. And yet, in the personalistic and institutionally fragile political systems of Kenya and Tanzania, public policy has as yet proved unable to perform its essential role. Part of the reason for this shortcoming lies in the historical legacy of colonialism, which helped to create the present ecological discontinuities while failing also to establish decision making and administrative mechanisms for their amelioration. The basic poverty of the two countries has contributed its own constraints. Also responsible is a fundamental separation of policy makers and their decisions from the societies which they seek to influence and shape. As Robert Jackson and Carl Rosberg have noted:

> One cannot understand the whys and wherefores of personal rule by focusing upon underlying socioeconomic factors because such factors are by themselves too general to guide political choices in personal regimes. In advanced societies...where the choices and actions of governments are far more significantly (but by no means exclusively) policy and technical choices—such conditions can be very influential, and a study of them is important. But in underdeveloped countries where politics is more about power than policy—and where success or failure in policy is much less likely to bring direct political rewards or losses—the relationship between ruling and the socioeconomic environment is much weaker.*

In spite of these obstacles, no substitute remains for effective public policy solutions to the ecological dilemmas today confronting Kenya, Tanzania, and the rest of Africa. The problems have simply become too large and widespread, and private initiatives are simply too weak, uncoordinated, and at times mutually contradictory. This study proceeds under the assumption that public policy can rise to this critical occasion, once the political will is found to accomplish the task.

Several organizations and many individuals have helped us in our work. We wish first to thank the West Virginia University Department of Political Science and the Environmental Studies Program at Dartmouth College for their financial and logistical support. Considerable encouragement and advice was provided by representatives of the Ford Foundation and the United Nations Environment Programme in Nairobi, and especially by Goran Hyden, David Jones, Peter Thacker, and Mona

* Robert H. Jackson and Carl G. Rosberg, *Personal Rule in Black Africa* (Berkeley: University of California Press, 1982), p. 75.

Bjorklund. The College of Agriculture and the International Rural Development Program of the University of Vermont afforded us an opportunity to present our preliminary findings at a March 1984 colloquium, "Agricultural Development: Africa, An Action-Oriented Strategy." Our thanks to Deans William Kelly and Robert Sinclair, and also to Robert Caiola and Jonathan Fisher, for including us in this important forum.

Generous financial assistance was granted to our project by the African-Caribbean Institute, which further helped us in preparing the research bibliography appended to this volume. We want, in particular, to acknowledge Meredeth Kendall for her efforts in sifting through a vast number of potential entries to this bibliography so that we could select only the most pertinent. We also appreciate the highly professional editorial services of Michele Martin, Nancy Sharlet, and their staffs at the State University of New York Press.

Finally, we owe much to the insights of the following people, who share our deep concern with Africa and all of its inhabitants: Michael Cockerell, Harvey Croze, Jan Geu Grootenhuis, Mark Halle, David Hopcraft, Saba Jallow, Hugh Lamprey, Robert Malpas, Esmond Martin, David Mbuve, Ellis Monks, Norman Myers, William Ntimama, Elisa Nyiti, James Shiorya Okete, Ian Parker, Scott Perkin, Fred Pertet, Sandra Price, G. R. Rogalsky, John Seago, David Sindeyo, James Thorsell, and David Western.

Being tempted, as always, to attribute any factual and interpretive errors to each other, we have agreed to assume joint responsibility for whatever inadequacies may remain in this book.

Rodger Yeager
Norman N. Miller

Introduction

. . . we have to share our land with wild and dangerous animals. We have to learn to give way to the elephant, the rhinocerous, the lion, etc., and this has not been our way of life.
> Maasai game warden relating a lament of the northern Kenyan Samburu people, quoted in Peter Matthiessen, *The Tree Where Man Was Born.*

He gave all he possessed for the wild animals of Africa, including his life.
> Inscription on a monument to naturalist Michael Grzimek, who is buried on the rim of Ngorongoro Crater, Tanzania.

Wild animals represent a mixed blessing for eastern Africa. On the one hand, the region's broad expanses of savanna and woodland provide the largest surviving refuge for the African continent's dwindling populations of untamed herbivores and carnivores. To all but the most insensitive—and the most desperate—this "last place on earth"[1] offers a final opportunity, and thus a powerful scientific and social obligation, to preserve its fauna and their habitats. In that scarcity enhances value, wild-

1

1   Cheetah cubs on a tourist vehicle, Nairobi National Park. Mark Bolton and World Wildlife Fund.

life also furnish an important source of wealth for impoverished countries that control few profitable resources. In various ways, affluent societies are prepared to translate the principle of ecological stewardship into a sound business proposition.

But wildlife bring problems as well as advantages to the human societies whose land they share. Tanzania and Kenya lie in the heart of eastern Africa and have become, quite literally, the last places on earth for some animal species. However, these countries are also experiencing two of the world's highest rates of population growth, urbanization, and incipient rural overcrowding. The majority of Kenyans and Tanzanians are precariously engaged in subsistence agriculture and, in relation to their limited technologies, are densely settled in zones of relatively high natural arability. Urban dwellers depend heavily on whatever food surpluses can be extracted from this subsistence "sector." Never very great, surpluses have become increasingly meager and unpredictable because of adverse weather and poor economic conditions, and also because of public policy failures related to the direct and indirect effects of population growth. As a result of these same factors, food shortages are now becoming regular occurrences in some of the more as well as less fertile rural areas.

It is entirely possible that, under existing agrotechnical, socioeconomic, and political circumstances, the human carrying capacity of eastern Africa will soon be exceeded; yet the aggregate population of Tanzania and Kenya will double in less than twenty years.[2] Unless these conditions are quickly altered, the only chance for expanding subsistence activity may include opening lands now reserved for wildlife. These reaches of grassland, bush, and forest were originally set aside over the protest of local farming and pastoral communities. To lessen conflict, areas to be evacuated were selected partly on the basis of their light population densities, which resulted, of course, from their agricultural marginalities. Rapid environmental destruction can therefore be anticipated from the simple conversion of these areas into high-density farms and livestock ranges, culminating in an eventual net loss not only of wildlife but also of food production and human life.

Especially when they arise in food-deficient and economically underdeveloped societies, questions of wildlife protection and land use are inherently political. Because of their wide impact and their potential for open hostility, such issues demand the kinds of carefully planned, authoritatively sanctioned, and uniformly administered policy responses

2 The emerging confrontation: wildlife, livestock, and fences on the eastern African savannah. David Keith Jones.

that cannot be expected from private initiatives alone. The present study approaches these themes as they appear in the policy experiences of Tanzania and Kenya. Tanzania has committed more territory to wildlife protection than has Kenya, in spite of the fact that Kenya has attracted the largest number of highly vocal nongovernmental organizations, funding groups, and individuals devoted to wildlife protection.

The following discussion examines a critically important policy dilemma yet to receive an adequate amount of scholarly and official attention. The study's major objective for both countries is to explain the singular urgency of the agricultural land-use problem as it applies to wildlife areas. For Kenya, an additional purpose is to explore the most pressing social and political issues of game management in this society's wildlife-oriented, but also land-hungry, policy environment.

The subjects at hand involve matters of life and death for animal species and human cultures that occupy spaces where the man-land-wildlife relationship is particularly intimate. From the broader perspective of history and from the contemporary record, we argue that the impending ecological collapses must largely be attributed to private misdirections and public policy errors concerning agricultural land use and wildlife protection. An accumulation of these mistakes has created situations that are today as destructive of indigenous ecosystems as they are developmentally counterproductive. Moreover, actions to improve land use and to defend wildlife have been taken that casually disregard their reciprocal effects. Many intervening variables have been ignored, and few problems have been resolved in relation to each other. Integrated policy making, implementation, and evaluation have taken back seats to disjointed incrementalism and erratic crisis intervention within and between the two issue areas.

Much of the reason for all these difficulties lies in a conspicuous absence of applied research and political commitment, a deficiency that must be overcome if Kenya and Tanzania are to achieve their developmental goals while avoiding environmental disaster and the extinction of their endangered wild animals. The study concludes with estimates of present directions and policy requirements in land-use and wildlife management.

———————————— 1 ————————————

Land Use and Wildlife in Eastern African History: Creating a Policy Problem

Introduction

Like most of its other developmental problems, eastern Africa's land-use and wildlife issues are neither historically unprecedented nor lacking in past solutions. These issues were addressed by the traditional segmentary societies that proliferated in the region before the imposition of European colonial rule. Colonialism nullified these accommodations, however, and helped create serious ecological imbalances that persist to this day. The purposes of this chapter are first to distinguish between the governing imperatives of precolonial and colonial public policy systems, and then to examine how the man-land-wildlife relationship was stabilized and subsequently upset in the earlier policy experiences of Tanzania and Kenya.

The Traditional and Colonial Policy Milieus

To a very large extent, the ecological harmony that emerged in precolonial times resulted from the policy requirements of traditional African societies. Confronting a challenging physical environment with the tools of iron-age technologies, indigenous cultures placed high value on consensus and cooperation in the daily affairs of life. In the political systems of these cultures, public policies derived more from popular consultation and discussion than from legislation and executive action. Policy implementation and adjudication were likewise carried out more through collective self-help than through formal bureaucratic and judicial processes. Individuals were commonly selected to represent the interests of a community's major kinship and age groups, and chiefly authority was exercised to varying degrees. Secret societies and other specially designated organizations often undertook specific tasks. But as in other parts of Africa, collective survival and prosperity favored consensual policy processes. Public opinion heavily influenced the deliberations of elders and age-grade councils, and the behavior of chiefs, religious spokesmen, and associational groups was held closely accountable to the public will.

Social and political organizations extended upward from nuclear and extended families to wider and deeper descent groups. Consensual policymaking and administrative principles applied regardless of whether the society was forged from a small and inclusive collection of extended families or from some larger amalgam of three- to four-generation lineages. At each constituent level, under these circumstances, "all disputes, all solutions, all agreements are hammered out between segments whose power is 'equivalent' and who are balanced against one another."[1] Even in communities containing one dominant lineage and others that were subordinate, political competition over scarce resources was managed through negotiations and compromises among all the different lineages represented in the territorial unit.

Segmentation and physical dispersion enhanced the stability of traditional policy processes by providing mechanisms for controlled and environmentally suitable change. Political authority above the homestead level was typically exercised by the elder representatives of the lineages making up each residential unit. These units contained segments of the larger descent groups, forming, in effect, microcosms of all the lineages segmentally distributed among several independent communities. Every segment possessed its own lineage geneology, and intersegment relations were maintained through exogamy and cooperative patterns of interaction. Bonds of kinship and cooperation integrated lineage segments and complemented the community's common culture of language, values, and beliefs. As explained by Middleton and Tait:

> Rights in resources and the exercise of authority must be distributed within local and descent groups, which can persist in time only so long as this distribution is accepted by all members. Conflict of interests is countered by various institutions that provide for the affirmation of joint as against sectional interests. This seems largely to depend upon non-empirical factors, which include a common God or body of ancestors to whom constituent units and their representatives feel responsibility for their actions, and a common mythology. These affirm both common bonds and the values on which right mutual behavior is based. Most potential conflicts of interests are limited by the common acceptance of social values of the members of society, rather than by legal or other sanctions that come into operation only after conflict has been actualized.[2]

When competition could not be managed in this manner, or when land shortages were experienced that could not be accommodated with existing technologies, lineage segments simply split from the community and migrated to new territory. This process effectively resolved otherwise insurmountable differences and allowed for an expansion of society while preserving its basic structural integrity and environmental adaptability. Segmentation and migration also produced cycles of recurrent change that help account for the remarkable durability of traditional policy systems. Destabilizing changes tended to occur only when unfavorable conditions prevented the establishment of new communities through out-migration. In the presence of unresolvable conflicts of interest, factors such as land shortages and external enemies could lead to political instability and to a breakdown in the policy procedures that integrated society. Such dislocations were relatively rare, however, and the practices of social segmentation and migration explain how most of Tanzania and Kenya were settled and politically organized before colonialism entered the scene. Opportunities offered by self-regenerating kinship structures and adequate amounts of arable land made it unnecessary to invent more complex and therefore less democratic forms of government, kept traditional societies demographically small, and helped keep them in close touch with the environment that supported their numbers. Today it is impossible to estimate precisely how traditional societies might have evolved, because events in the nineteenth century transformed a profusion of policy systems into a single, basic type—colonial.

Kenya was brought under British colonial rule in 1895 and was granted its independence in 1963. Germany governed mainland Tanzania between 1891 and 1919, when it surrendered control to the British following World War I. Britain administered the mainland as Tanganyika Territory until 1961 and continued its occupation of Zanizbar and Pemba islands, initiated in 1890, until 1963. In 1964, the mainland was united with the islands to form the United Republic of Tanzania.

Despite their several differences, Tanzanian and Kenyan colonial processes shared an important trait. On the widest scale imaginable, they exploited without restoring the natural and human treasures of eastern Africa. German and British policy systems enabled small alien minorities to destroy traditional patterns of political authority, cultural autonomy, and environmental adaptability. In an economic sense, the European presence was specifically designed to extract land, labor, and produce, to convert these resources into expatriated profit, and to exact further tribute by taxing local subjects to pay for their own administration and by addicting them to the cheap export products of industrial Europe. African ecosystems were ruthlessly subjected to these goals, with disasterous effects in Tanzania and with even graver long-term consequences for a Kenya endowed with comparatively abundant exploitable resources and saddled with a larger European population.

Tanzanian and Kenyan colonial experiences are generally discussed in two of the authors' other works.[3] The concern here is with the ecological imbalance in human and animal land use that had been controlled in traditional eastern Africa, was revived and intensified during the colonial period, and has now reached crisis levels in those places where people and wildlife still compete for the same space.

The Tanzanian Experience

Two assumptions have commonly been accepted about the man-land-wildlife relationship in precolonial Tanzania.[4] The first is that people and wild animals lived in a state of distant and consequently harmonious co-existence. The second conjecture is that this symbiosis was actually promoted by local wars and by the African slave trade, said to have depopulated large areas by the middle to late nineteenth century. From his careful reconstruction of Tanzanian history, Kjekshus argues that both these suppositions are false. He maintains that until colonialism inserted its decisive controls, conflict typified the human-wildlife nexus.[5] Further, a dualistic approach to land use had evolved by this time, which insured a stable to slowly growing human population while helping to limit the proliferation of wildlife.

In parts of the north, west, and south, relatively plentiful rainfall and fertile soils permitted dense rural populations, dispersed settlement patterns, and agricultural regimes featuring short-fallow, annual, and even multiple cropping on individually managed plots. Here, as in similar regions of Kenya, a wide variety of food and trade crops was grown with the aid of innovations such as irrigation, crop rotation and intercropping, manuring, legume-based nitrogen fixing, and anti-erosion field techniques. Nucleated and widely spaced villages predominated in many of the less arable and lightly populated frontier localities. Here concentrated settlements were encouraged by the presence of predators and because communally organized grazing and constantly shifting cultivation were required to compensate for low rainfall and poor soil quality. This land-extensive, agricultural "periphery" effectively protected the intensively cultivated, agricultural "center" by holding at bay the worst effects of the resident wildlife.

> The prosperity of the centre depended in a remarkable way on the control of the periphery. . . . Even a relatively small population at the periphery of the human settlement could neutralize the fauna and keep under control the dangerous combination of trypanosomes, their hosts (wildlife) and their vectors (tsetse flies) which in later decades became the major obstacle to development in large parts of the country.[6]

1.1 Eastern Africa's agricultural periphery. Rodger Yeager.

A gradually expanding agricultural periphery meant that tsetse-infested bushlands were geographically smaller in precolonial times than today, and that the sparsely populated eastern African cattle complex was reciprocally larger. The continuing process of social segmentation/dispersion insured that an ecological equilibrium was maintained to the advantage of peripheral African societies, while not threatening wildlife populations with extinction.

Kjekshus' interpretation finds theoretical support in an earlier study by Boserup,[7] which rejected the Malthusian hypothesis that rapid population growth must always subject subsistence societies to progressive environmental deterioration and eventual food shortages. She contended that under favorable climatic and soil conditions, high human fertility and rising population densities will lead to an intensification of land use and farm labor and to the adoption of technical innovations that retain soil quality while increasing agricultural productivity. Without these improvements, shortened fallow periods would quickly exhaust the land, terminally reduce crop yields, and leave no alternative to starvation except long-distance migration beyond the optimal limits of segmentation.[8]

In less manageable ecosystems, low-density populations tend to employ land-extensive agricultural practices that necessitate fewer inputs of labor and technology. Owing to their long fallow periods, these practices incur little environmental damage that is not self-corrective. Deprived of the opportunity and incentive to intensify production, however, societies engaged in extensive cropping are trapped in a "vicious circle of sparse population and primitive technology," in which "with a system of long fallow and with abundant land and little input of agricultural labour, the cultivated area is often barely sufficient to give a crop which can last until the following harvest."[9] Similar limitations affect pastoral groups and the grasslands over which they range.

In summary, the probable connection between wildlife and land use in traditional Tanzania confined game and other wild animals to a slowly shrinking domain that still lay beyond the needs and capacities of the animals' most immediate human competitors. These pioneers of the agricultural periphery lived in scattered segmentary communities and struggled to make ends meet, while inadvertently providing a mutually protective buffer that separated the fauna from densely settled pockets of intensive agricultural activity. From the moment of its imposition, colonialism destroyed this dynamic and somewhat unstable balance.

The 1890s and early 1900s were years of deep turmoil for Tanzania. The consolidation of German colonial rule inflicted three disasters on unsuspecting and unprepared indigenous societies: epidemics of smallpox, rinderpest, and other diseases that decimated human and livestock populations; colonial "pacification" campaigns followed by World War I, which further depopulated large parts of the country; and European confiscations of land, crops, and African labor, which produced famines and upset delicate subsistence equilibria that had taken centuries to evolve. One purpose of land alienation was heralded in a colonial ordinance of 1896 that created two hunting reserves in northern and eastern Tanzania. The Germans later increased the number of these reserves before German imperialism was banished from Africa in 1919.

Assuming formal administrative control in 1922, the British added new reserves and eventually extended the game reserve concept to include the removal of people from locations considered essential to wildlife protection. The first evacuations were actually conducted to curb sleeping sickness epidemics that resulted from the spread of wildlife and their tsetse parasites after the initial devastation of Tanzania's agricultural periphery. Other movements were intended to free lands of high potential for European commercial agriculture. Trypanosomiasis, combined with a growing European and African demand for land, led to pressure for the total elimination of wild animals. In response to this threat and to a significant rise in poaching, game preservationists intensified their efforts on behalf of wildlife protection. Their lobbying brought about a further extension of depopulated game areas and contributed to the establishment of national parks, in which both settlement and hunting were prohibited.[10]

Thus were introduced two policy conceptions that yet prevail in modern Tanzania—consolidating local populations for economic and social reasons and denying the settlement of large tracts, set aside as game sanctuaries. These ideas translated into an abandonment of the agricultural periphery to the wildlife, creating "a frontier situation where the conquest of the ecosystem had to recommence."[11] The struggle has not ceased, as man and animals continue to vie for survival in an arena shrinking for them both.

In a previous time the frontline of human settlement was employed as an agricultural commons, in which low population densities and limited technologies worked to preserve an imperfect but viable harmony of land use and animal life. The events of this century have transformed a rough symmetry of the commons into a tragedy,[12] where increasing densities have outstripped technological capacities. Raising the Malthusian specter for humans and enhancing the probability of extinction for many wild species, the Tanzanian version of this tragedy is heavily related to public policy decisions. Only through public policy reforms can the Tanzanian commons be saved so that native life forms, impoverished peasant communities, and a compressed agricultural center will be protected against the ravages of a periphery now out of control.

The Kenyan Experience

Essentially the same historical processes that occurred in Tanzania also affected Kenya, except that in Kenya a much larger European presence further reduced the available land for Africans and increased the survival risks for game animals. Most of the naturally arable land lies in the southwest quadrant of Kenya. Here is where the precolonial agricultural center was located and where traditional segmentary societies were the most numerous. Here too is where white settlers established their farms as Britain extended its colonial reach over what became known as the Kenyan "white highlands." With the consolidation of colonial rule, Europeans travelled over Kenya for more sporting reasons. A hunter's diary from 1928 reported that "we shot 52 lions today...perhaps overdoing it a bit."

Early European settlers expressed considerable ambiguity about wildlife and constantly debated the merits of animal conservation versus the right to hunt. The need to protect farm crops from animal pests was often cited in defense of indiscriminate shooting. For its part, the colonial administration had as its first priority the encouragement of an economic system featuring European commercial agriculture. As all manner of wildlife began to disappear, however, international pressure mounted for policies that would protect the most endangered species. The British colonial office responded by mandating that Kenya follow South Africa's lead and designate game reserve areas where hunting would be licensed. The South African authorities had created the continent's first reserve in 1895, and Kenya followed suit in 1896. As in Tanzania, the Kenyan reserves were not placed in the heavily settled agricultural center, but rather in the drier peripheral regions and in a few better-watered places of perennial competition between pastoralists and game animals. Also in common with Tanzania, it was the technologically least adaptable African societies that were compelled to make room for the new game sanctuaries.

The Kenya reserves proliferated until eighteen were eventually gazetted. Yet, by the middle 1940s it had already become apparent that they were inadequate for guarding wildlife against an insatiable European and African demand for land, against the depredations of poachers and the ecological disturbances caused by hunters and tourists, and against the deep-seated African perception of wild animals as annoying and dangerous vermin. Indigenous opposition to the alienation of game land came to a head at Amboseli, a plentiful wildlife habitat of 3,276 square kilometers (1,260 square miles) extending west from the base of Mt. Kilimanjaro. Originally part of a grazing area allocated to the pastoral Maasai, well-watered Amboseli had traditionally attracted large numbers of herders and their livestock. At the urging of conservationists, the colonial government sought to protect Amboseli's diminishing animal populations by enclosing them in a national park. The Maasai bitterly protested this move and also pointed out that large wild ungulate populations would spread disease among their cattle, even though the latter were restricted from the park.

In the face of this opposition, the administration converted Amboseli into a "park adjunct" (later termed a national reserve) and permitted limited Maasai access to the park's grass and water. The colonial administration also attempted to place itself above the competition between land users and wildlife advocates by transferring supervisory control of Amboseli to the quasi-private Trustees of the Royal National Parks of Kenya. This action gave official status to wildlife preservationists and introduced yet another dimension to eastern Africa's man-land-wildlife disequilibrium.

In a manner similar to what happened in Tanzania, the Kenyan game reserves and national parks uprooted African subsistence communities, reduced the amount of land for their shifting cultivation and seminomadic pastoralism, and exposed crops and livestock to environmental dangers that had previously been curtailed at the periphery of human settlement. While these changes were taking place, human and animal population densities increased at comparable rates in both territories, as European land alienation proceeded, as African social segmentation and migration continued, and as game animals multiplied in their protected habitats. Unique to Kenya were the larger numbers of European settlers and the elevation of private wildlife interests to formal positions of power in the public sector. In their determination to preserve game animals at whatever cost to local societies, these spokesmen added an element of rigidity still present in the Kenyan debate over land and wildlife. As in Tanzania, this debate can only be resolved through public policy; but to a greater extent than in Tanzania, a profusion of special interest wildlife lobbies must also be accommodated in solutions to Kenya's tragedy of the commons for man, land, and animals.

The Historical Legacy

The Tanzanian and Kenyan experiences are not unique, and neither are their effects. Even where wildlife factors have not played a major role, similar historical episodes have helped set the stage for the kinds of degenerative phenomena that threaten survival and development throughout contemporary Africa. In the words of a recent World Bank assessment:

> Droughts have underlined the seriousness of soil erosion, deforestation, and fuelwood shortages. They are closely related problems. In many parts of Africa, traditional farming is used to maintain soil productivity and forest cover against a background of relatively stable populations. This balance has been upset by rapid population growth and rising demand for food crops and fuelwood (particularly from urban areas). Farmers and pastoralists have damaged the land by shortening the fallow period and extending the cultivated and grazed area. In many countries, forest cover is being irretrievably damaged, with appalling consequences for household fuel supplies, soil fertility, and water supply.[13]

According to World Bank estimates, fuelwood use currently exceeds new tree growth by a factor of two and one-half in Tanzania and by five in Kenya.

Such problems cannot solely be attributed to population growth and rising economic demand, but rather to a more complex inheritance of environmental exploitation and public policy neglect. To clarify its linkages with human and wildlife populations, this legacy can be divided into a chronological sequence of stages that has produced much hardship in the peripheral farming, pastoral, and game areas of modern Kenya and Tanzania.

STAGE 1

Characteristics: Rapid increases in population density at the periphery of human settlement lead to declining agricultural carrying capacities and to growing land shortages. Shifting peasant cultivation is replaced by short-fallow and permanent cropping at pre-existing levels of technology. Pastoralists experience restricted grazing opportunities. Export crops are introduced in more fertile locations and partly replace food crops. Land scarcity, a shrinking pastoral commons, and pressure for human expansion into productively marginal wildlife areas result in lobbying efforts by wildlife activists and other conservationists. Policy decisions are made to create and expand wildlife refuges.

This stage began during the colonial period and extended through independence. The ecological irrationalities it yielded were largely ignored by Kenyan and Tanzanian policy elites, who were preoccupied after independence with consolidating their rule and with implementing ambitious development strategies. Unfortunately for both countries, many of the policies selected to achieve these goals actually worsened the problems of population density, land hunger, and environmental depletion initiated under colonialism. A growing crisis in land use ensued, abetted by public policy. The details of this situation are discussed in chapters 2 and 3. Here they are outlined in the remaining stages of a scenario that could have been proposed by Thomas Malthus.

STAGE 2

Characertistics: Postindependence development programs extend governmental control over the Kenyan and Tanzanian economies, encourage export over food crops, and provide improved health services but not significantly increased investments in agricultural technology, credit, and other services. Additional land is allocated to wildlife sanctuaries. For the Tanzanian society, public sector involvement in the rural areas includes an enforced but essentially unplanned and technically unsupported movement of virtually the entire population into concentrated villages. The efficiently administered rural development assistance that was to justify this massive relocation fails to materialize. In the food crop sectors of both countries, producer prices are lowered to subsidize growing numbers of impoverished urban dwellers. Food shortages begin to appear that are related to public policy decisions as well as to migration and weather. Increasing landlessness and inequality in the countryside drive yet more people into the towns and cities. Food imports become periodically necessary to feed burgeoning urban populations. At the agricultural periphery, competition intensifies among land users and between them and indigenous wildlife species.

As urban centers continue to grow in population and in their dependency on food-producing rural areas, the latter are subjected to ecological disturbances that Paul Harrison has detected in many parts of tropical Africa. In their eastern African manifestations, these tragedies of the commons are significantly related to a policy of benign neglect in

Kenyan rural development and to much more extensive but developmentally inadequate policy interventions in Tanzania.

> Everywhere in Africa, as population has grown, fallow periods—essential for the restoration of soil fertility—have shrunk. Farmers are returning to the same patch of ground too frequently, so yields fall and the soil is exhausted, sometimes irrevocably. Modern agricultural methods could compensate for this: ploughing would turn up the deeper layers of soil and enable a patch to be cultivated longer. With adequate use of fertilizer or manure, an area can be cultivated permanently. But most African farmers are still using the old methods without ploughs or fertilizer. They are practicing settled agriculture with the technology of shifting cultivation. They are trying to support an increasingly dense population with methods suited for a scattered one. This contradiction, more than anything else, lies at the bottom of Africa's ecological predicament and her endemic poverty.[14]

In a physical setting that encourages higher and higher rates of social segmentation and migration, human fertility and population growth reinforce this Malthusian dilemma. As lineages disperse in search of still arable land and "as populations continue to grow and there is no extra land to bring into cultivation, the only solution people can see is to migrate. Some of them move into the free areas that are left, and they are often free because they are difficult to work or even more ecologically precarious than the places people came from."[15] In Tanzania and in Kenya, such areas encompass the broad and environmentally vulnerable expanses presently reserved for wildlife.

STAGE 3

Characteristics: Unprecedented human population densities are reached in the less arable settled areas in the vicinity of unsettled ecosystems into which wildlife are compressed. Continued lobbying by wildlife advocates, unabated reductions in agricultural carrying capacity, and additional local land shortages result from these population pressures. Sedentary village communities remain condemned to practice permanent cultivation and limited-range grazing at inadequate levels of technology, investment, and productivity to guarantee reliable subsistence offtakes, let alone to produce food surpluses. A further shrinking of the agricultural commons is caused by rapid environmental deterioration involving soil exhaustion, erosion, and the disappearance of trees and grasses. A tendency develops for peasants to withdraw into purely subsistence cultivation and black-market trade in food products. Fewer officially marketed food crops are grown, and urban food shortages become chronic. Economic inequalities widen between less arable and more arable rural locations, stimulating new waves of rural-to-urban migration and pauperization. Permanent ecological damage is caused by environmentally excessive wildlife population densities, by movements of humans and livestock into agriculturally unsuitable lands that directly border wildlife areas, and by surges in food- and profit-related game poaching.

STAGE 4

Characteristics: The agricultural periphery becomes still more densely settled, placing the legally sanctioned wildlife refuges at direct risk and threatening ecological collapse for all their inhabitants.

To summarize the historical legacy that must now be confronted in Kenya and Tanzania, before game animals were viewed as valuable and endangered natural resources, unstable but mutually beneficial ecological balances were maintained between land users and wildlife species. Each group helped prevent the demographic expansion of the other beyond what the physical environment could support. The animal's most immediate competitors lived in widely scattered and intermittently mobile settlements and practiced shifting cultivation and seminomadic herding at low levels of technology, productivity, and environmental disturbance.

During the early colonial period, policy choices were made to establish game parks and reserves, to encourage commercial agriculture, and later to satisfy basic human needs. The net results of these precedents were rapidly growing rural populations and population densities in the agriculturally peripheral areas adjacent to the newly designated wildlife preserves. Population pressures also mounted in the parks and reserves, as wide-ranging, large ungulates were now confined to finite spaces, a condition of being protected. Intense partisanship by wildlife preservationists led to an expansion of these sanctuaries, incidentally preventing systematic culling operations to maintain pre-existing animal balances per unit of land.

What has happened since threatens both people and animals with a devolutionary spiral of overpopulation and declining subsistence. In general, reduced agricultural carrying capacities have accompanied rising rural population densities and sedentary settlement patterns. Farmers are forced, under these circumstances, to practice short-fallow and permanent cultivation using technologies designed for bush cultivation and long-fallow cropping with rotational cycles of up to many years in some places. At the agricultural periphery, the presence of protected game areas has also meant a contracting game and livestock commons, steadily growing populations of wild and domesticated animals, and increasing loss of forage and animal quality to overgrazing and soil depletion. Combined with development orientations that neglect the agricultural periphery and replace food crops with export crops in the agricultural center, these assaults on fragile ecosystems have contributed to a permanent loss of arable land, to regular food shortages, to greater rural landlessness and inequality, to higher rates of urban immigration, and to a consequent dependence on grain imports and restricted producer prices—both of which worsen the urban subsistence problem by further reducing domestic food output.

As Boserup earlier observed, these outcomes are not inevitable from simple population growth. Rather, they arise from successive policy choices that have acted to enlarge rural, urban, and wildlife population densities while failing also to enhance rural carrying capacities and to improve agricultural productivity. From the standpoint of all species caught in its thrall, however, a policy-related Malthusian crisis is just as lethal as if it had occurred in nature. The following chapters explore the factors surrounding this emergency as it unfolds in contemporary Tanzania and Kenya.

2

Land Use and Wildlife in Modern Tanzania

RODGER YEAGER

Introduction

In the Malthusian-like dialectic outlined in the preceding chapter, ecological tragedies of the commons result from consistent failures in agricultural development policy accompanied by human encroachments into eastern Africa's surviving natural ecosystems, including its wildlife refuges. Financially constrained as they are, the agricultural and natural resource policies of independent Tanzania have recently sought to reverse these trends, with international tourism providing a pecuniary incentive to succeed. In reference to the famous Ngorongoro Crater, for example, the 1976–1981 national development plan stated that "the Ngorongoro Conservation Authority will have the responsibility of administering and conserving natural resources with the purpose of developing tourism, making scientific researches, effecting a balance between man and his environment, conserving soil, and conserving natural resources for the

21

benefit of future generations."[1] To appreciate how and to what extent these aspirations are not being realized (including in the physically enclosed and thus easily monitored Ngorongoro Crater), it is necessary first to examine the general consequences of national development policy and then to explore those parts of the Tanzanian agricultural periphery where national policy has had its greatest impact on human society and wildlife species.

National Policy Influences

Colonial and postcolonial governments enclosed lands for commercial agriculture in the wetter and more fertile rural areas of Tanzania and for wildlife protection in the drier peripheral regions. Public health programs and educational campaigns were also mounted, which quickly reduced infant and child mortality. As Table 2.1 indicates, the long-term consequences of these policies included not only a rapid growth in population and population density, but likewise a steady increase in the *rates* of this growth. By the time of the most recent national census in 1978,

Table 2.1. Mainland Tanzanian Population Growth, 1948–1978

Census Year	Total Population	Estimated Average Annual Growth Rate (%)	Average Density (per km²)
1948	7,981,120	–	9.04
1957	9,600,852	2.25	10.87
1967	11,958,654	2.82	13.54
1978	17,048,329	3.30	19.30

NOTE: The data suggest an average annual growth rate of 3.85 percent between 1967 and 1978. The Tanzanian director of census questioned this statistic, guessing that it underestimated the country's crude death rate during this period. The official census report accepts an estimated average annual growth rate of 3.30 percent, and adds that "due to better preparations in the 1978 census and the almost total villagization of the country, facilitating enumeration, it is the impression that the coverage in 1978 was better than in 1967" (Tanzania, *1978 Population Census*, p. 34).

SOURCES: Tanzania, *Statistical Abstract, 1965* (Dar es Salaam: Central Statistical Bureau, Ministry of Economic Affairs and Development Planning, 1967), p. 10; and Tanzania, *1978 Population Census Preliminary Report* (Dar es Salaam: Bureau of Statistics, Ministry of Finance and Planning, n.d.), p. 177.

a pattern had emerged that is suggested in Figures 2.1 and 2.2. Administrative regions of greater annual rainfall experienced higher growth rates and densities, while regions of lower annual rainfall displayed lower densities but growth rates either equalling or exceeding the national average.

Neither the colonial nor independent governments matched their public health initiatives with equally effective measures to raise agricultural productivity and food sufficiency. Following their assumption of power in 1961, African political elites announced their determination to overcome the production losses and environmental deterioration that were exacerbated by rural overcrowding and a lack of agricultural devel-

Fig. 2.1. Regional Population Growth and Density in Tanzania, 1978

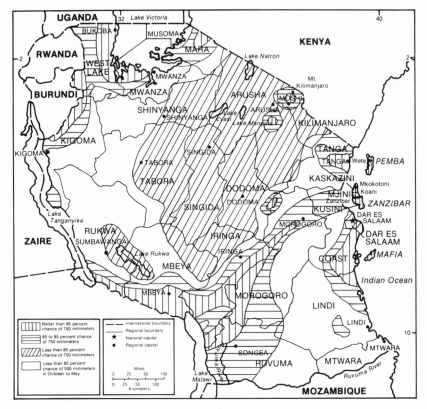

Fig. 2.2. Annual Rainfall Probabilities in Tanzania

opment assistance. They estimated that if these objectives were to be reached, large numbers of peasants would have to be moved from scattered homesteads and isolated villages into concentrated and easily accessible farming centers. An early attempt at villagization failed by 1966 because of its excessive capital costs and its unexpected tendency to transform relatively self-reliant farmers into economically dependent and demanding *kulaks*.[2] In 1967, after the Arusha Declaration had committed Tanzania to rural socialism and self-reliance, the party-government adopted a policy of relocating peasants into self-help socialist villages. The regime underestimated the practical difficulty of

2.1   The communal ideal that failed. Tanzania Ministry of Agriculture.

combining resettlement with an immediate transition to communal production and income distribution, and in 1973 modified the *ujamaa vijijini*
(socialism in the villages) mandate to emphasize the speedy villagization
and eventual communalization of virtually the entire rural society.[3]

The results were impressive. Following a massive campaign of persuasion, economic inducement, and outright force, by 1977 more than 90
percent of the peasantry reportedly resided in about 7,300 villages at an
average occupancy of over 1,000 inhabitants per village.[4] The impact of
this huge exercise in directed migration was not felt equally in all parts of
the country, and today about 60 percent of the resettled population lives
in areas of low rainfall prone to density-related ecological problems.
Here too are situated some of the largest and most important wildlife
areas.

Table 2.2 distinguishes among the three types of Tanzanian wildlife
sanctuaries. Together, national parks, game reserves, and game con-

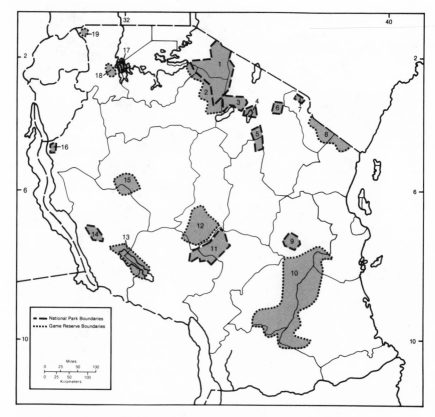

Fig. 2.3. Tanzanian National Parks and Major Game Reserves

Park and Reserve Names in Figure 2.3

1.	Serengeti National Park	11.	Ruaha National Park
2.	Maswa Game Reserve	12.	Rungwa River Game Reserve
3.	Ngorongoro Conservation Area	13.	Uwanda Game Reserve
4.	Lake Manyara National Park	14.	Katavi Plain National Park
5.	Tarangire National Park	15.	Ugalla River Game Reserve
6.	Arusha National Park	16.	Gombe Stream National Park
7.	Kilimanjaro National Park	17.	Rubondo Island National Park
8.	Mkomazi Game Reserve	18.	Biharamulo Game Reserve
9.	Mikumi National Park	19.	Rumanyika Orugundu Game
10.	Selous Game Reserve		Reserve

NOTE: There are also nine other game reserves and fifty game controlled areas. National parks and game reserves are managed by the national government, while controlled areas are administered by regional authorities.

Table 2.2. Types of Tanzanian Wildlife Areas

Type	Number	Area (km²)	Percent Mainland Tanzania
National Parks and Conservation Areas (hunting prohibited, settlement generally prohibited)	11	40,229	5
Game Reserves (hunting by limited permit, settlement generally prohibited)	17	83,450	9
Game Controlled Areas (hunting by limited permit, settlement generally permitted)	50	122,910	14

trolled areas account for approximately 28 percent of the country's total area and for a much higher proportion of the environmentally delicate zones where nucleated agricultural communities are most abundant. Wildlife advocates had originally hoped that closely gathered villages would benefit game animals by preserving and even extending the vast open spaces many of these species require. This benefit has not come to pass, however, because the settlements have not received sufficient development assistance to guarantee their survival as sedentary agricultural communities employing intensive land-use techniques.

THE AGRICULTURAL LAND-USE PREDICAMENT

We have argued elsewhere that the Tanzanian party-government has been more successful in resettling rural dwellers than in providing for their basic productive needs.[5] Between 1967 and 1982, neither the nationalization of major economic activities nor an administrative decentralization of government proved enough to compensate for an absence of producer price incentives, rural credit, fertilizers, and extension services. Also ignored were improvements in agricultural marketing, transport, and storage, as well as mechanisms to restore and maintain soil fertility such as small-scale irrigation, crop rotation, and reforestation. By 1980–

1982, per capita food output had fallen to about 88 percent of the level established between 1969 and 1971.[6]

Although adverse weather played some part, responsibility for these lapses cannot be assigned to population growth. As Boserup has in fact argued:

> It is true of many kinds of public investment that they are determined by the size of the area more than by the number of inhabitants. An increase in population reduces the per capita costs of such investments and services in rural areas, and this advantage is likely to be so large that it can more than offset the relatively light burden of some additional agricultural investment. For this reason, even rapid and prolonged population increase . . . seems more likely to be a blessing than a curse, if the political problems connected with land tenure and the technical problems connected with soil erosion can be solved.[7]

The political problem of land tenure was eased by the decision to postpone communalization. In addition to poor weather and the international economic recession of recent years, the real reasons for Tanzania's flagging agricultural performance lie in a pattern of inadequate investment in the rural areas, especially in those areas that produce food crops, combined with policy-induced land-use practices that are economically irrational and environmentally destructive.

Within the limitations of an essentially nationalized economic system burdened with high administrative costs, Tanzanian planners are engaged in a constant struggle to balance growth with equity. Based on spending estimates and projections from 1980, Table 2.3 discloses a changing emphasis in development funding from industry to economic infrastructure and education. The table also indicates a consistently low financial priority attached to agriculture. The party-government sought productive diversification in the immediate post-villagization period and, at the same time, tried to complete its ambitious educational and social welfare programs. In an effort to free investment capital for these purposes, the leadership instructed the agricultural sector essentially to develop itself. The 1976–1981 development plan acknowledged the Arusha Declaration's call for rural self-reliance by directing that "a big part of agricultural production does not require government investment and hence will be implemented through the farmer's own efforts."[8] In an

Table 2.3. Tanzanian Development Expenditures, 1976–1990
(percent of totals estimated and projected in 1980)

Sector	1976–1981 Projections	1976–1979 Expenditures	1981–1990 Projections
Agriculture & Livestock	13.5	16.9	11.2
Industry	24.2	20.0	2.7
Natural Resources	1.4	1.2	1.2
Mining	3.5	3.5	3.4
Commerce & Tourism	1.2	1.1	1.0
Water	5.8	7.7	2.4
Power	4.7	3.5	6.0
Construction & Public Works	9.9	6.0	16.4
Transport & Communications	7.3	6.8	16.1
Education & Culture	7.9	5.9	34.7
Health	3.5	2.9	0.9
Administration	15.4	24.5	–[a]
Other	1.7	–	4.0
TOTAL	100.0	100.0	100.0

[a] Administrative service costs are not included in these projections. This omission leads to an underestimation of the planned reduction in agricultural expenditures in relation to less directly productive allocations.

SOURCES: Tanzanian and World Bank data compiled in Archibald R. M. Ritter, "Tanzania's Agricultural Sector: An Analysis of Past Performance and an Evaluation of the 1980–1981 Policy Initiatives," paper prepared for the Commonwealth Africa Division, Canadian International Development Agency, August 1981, p. 30.

economy dominated by subsistence farmers who need little more than the means for their own livelihood, this laissez faire attitude exerted a powerful negative influence on growth, equity, and national self-sufficiency in food.

Reflecting on the effects of these past policy decisions, the minister for planning and economic affairs later lamented: "We really thought that agriculture was like manna from heaven."[9] The party-government has since revised its priorities in favor of the agricultural sector, but not necessarily in favor of its food crop component. This policy shift, motivated by considerations of sheer economic survival in the 1980s, is further discussed in the concluding chapter.

Concerning land use, the villagization campaign was centered on subsistence areas of low potential for widespread cash-cropping. Several factors help to explain this focus, including an official reluctance to disrupt export production and a greater willingness of poorer farmers to be moved. Accordingly, local resettlement officers often took the course of least resistance and filled their quotas with people who used a shifting land-use pattern as a necessary environmental adaptation.[10] An upshot of this special attention paid to peripheral farming regions was that completely immovable and densely populated villages now dotted the landscapes adjoining Tanzania's major wildlife areas.

The speed and scope of resettlement inevitably meant that villages were hastily and sometimes poorly sited, so that they lacked access to basic amenities such as water and fuelwood. Given the available agricultural technologies, moreover, they were often too large for the carrying capacity of the land. The French agronomist René Dumont visited the rural areas in 1979. He observed a phenomenon in the Tanzanian countryside that Michael Chisholm had generally warned about: because many completely sedentary villages were so big and were placed so far from production plots, soil fertility was rapidly disappearing.[11]

Chisholm first described the justifications for shifting land-use practices in countries like Tanzania. Subsistence farmers prefer to settle on or near plots that offer the highest return on their labor, thereby reducing the costs of travel to their most productive fields. In a dispersed settlement committed to shifting cultivation, each farmer's land-use decisions will be determined by the varying quality of his land, and he will locate his homestead accordingly.[12] When choice is removed through the enclosure of peasants within large and heavily concentrated villages, the flexibility of dispersed settlement and widely spaced village residence is also lost. Under subsistence conditions, there is always a tendency for the best lands to be exploited beyond the limits of their fertility. Shifting cultivation normally protects these lands from permanent environmental damage, but "where the cultivators are sedentary, soil exhaustion, leading to erosion, may become a real menace on the nearer lands, threatening the whole economy of the settlement."[13] Dumont discovered extensive soil exhaustion and erosion barely two years after the completion of villagization.

Viewed from another perspective, officially marketed staple crops began their steep decline in 1973, as the villagization program gained its full momentum during one of the worst droughts in recent Tanzanian his-

2.2   The perils of villagizing the periphery: Hamwino Village, Dodoma Region, under drought conditions. Tanzanian Ministry of Agriculture.

tory.[14] Interestingly enough, total food production remains much higher than what is officially collected and sold. The failure of agricultural development policy to accommodate increasing rural population densities has also contributed to a situation in which growing numbers of peasants are exercising their "exit options"[15] of either withdrawing totally into subsistence farming or selling their surpluses on the black market where prices are higher than the official rates. Food shortages are becoming more frequent in the urban areas, which are intended to benefit from low producer prices and which continue to receive a steady stream of rural migrants.

Slackening agricultural production, spreading environmental degradation, and an average annual urbanization rate approaching 9 percent all give rise to an expanding demand for food imports, which in turn requires an uninterrupted flow of foreign exchange earnings. The critical need for hard currency, not the inherent value of wildlife, accounts for Tanzania's recent interest in its national parks and game reserves.

THE AMBIGUITIES OF WILDLIFE PROTECTION

Neither the wildlife refuges nor the tourist industry that helps support them received much official attention in the decade following the Arusha Declaration.[16] Falling agricultural productivity, deteriorating terms of trade, and chronic foreign exchange shortages have lately convinced policy makers to rethink the role of tourism in the Tanzanian economy. As the general manger of the Tanzania Tourist Corporation suggested in an outline of future policy, environmental protection is an unavoidable corollary to a viable tourist industry.

> We hope to make tourism the second or first most important earner of foreign exchange. To this end, we must extend our marketing abroad and educate our tour operators as much as possible. We intend first to develop the southern circuit, which includes the Selous and Mikumi game reserves, Dar es Salaam, and Zanzibar. Second, we shall move away from luxury hotels to a more economical and functional base. I would like to see a lot more local flavor and more local materials in use. Third, we are offering local subsidized programs so that our people can get to know and appreciate their own country and therefore feel more responsible for its preservation; otherwise poaching will only increase.[17]

Tourism came to a virtual standstill in 1977, beginning with the collapse of East African Airways Corporation and subsequently the entire East African Economic Community. A later closing of the border with Kenya, compounded by the general economic malaise and a short but unsettling war with Uganda, almost completely sealed Tanzania off from the Nairobi-based tourist trade.[18]

By 1979, steps were being taken to recapture some of this business. A single parastatal corporation had already replaced three separate and inefficiently managed tourist authorities. Lodging facilities were renovated and expanded with the help of a World Bank loan. The recently formed Air Tanzania Corporation established a somewhat whimsically maintained flight schedule between Dar es Salaam and Kilimanjaro International Airport, which serves the northern game parks. The reliability of this schedule improved when a $25 million Japanese bank loan enabled the purchase of two Boeing 737 aircraft. To provide the necessary external air links, Royal Dutch Airlines (KLM), British Airways, and

Ethiopian Airlines agreed to initiate direct flights to Kilimanjaro as well as to Nairobi and Dar es Salaam. As a result of these improvements, park visits increased from approximately 242,000 bed nights in 1979 to about 292,000 bed nights in 1980.

Less tractable problems have hampered the further development of tourism, including Tanzania's rudimentary road network, its lack of ground vehicles, spare parts, and fuel, and an average one-week supply of foreign exchange that eliminates the kinds of luxury consumables that tourists demand and must be imported. Another difficulty came to a head in July 1982, when eight Western airlines threatened to terminate all service to Tanzania because they were not reimbursed for local ticket sales. The Bank of Tanzania found sufficient hard currency to pay $1 million, about one-sixth of the total debt. In spite of such setbacks, by the early 1980s Tanzania was firmly back in the tourist business. The relative costs and benefits of this venture are as yet undetermined for either of its intended beneficiaries, the national development budget or the wildlife.

At the interface of tourism, agricultural development, and wildlife ecology, Tanzanian public policy is just as problematic and almost as poorly funded as is tourism alone. Extending a set of goals established under the second five-year plan, the third plan set seven local objectives for wildlife for the period of 1976 to 1981. Although not yet implemented, they continue to define the directly productive role expected from wildlife in Tanzanian rural development.

(a) Construction of roads, water wells and other service facilities in game controlled areas where such services are nonexistent.

(b) Improving upon such facilities where they are already existing.

(c) Guarding against poaching.

(d) Protection of people, farms and livestock in places bordering game controlled areas.

(e) Advancing game cropping programmes for the provision of game meat, especially in livestock meat-deficient areas.

(f) Promotion of horns/tusks curio-making on a collective basis.

(g) Giving guidance to villagers in starting hunting cooperatives.[19]

These activities are to be financed and administered at the regional level of government, where national policy and development administration are supposed to meet. They apply only to game controlled areas, the protected zones that permit the greatest amount of private interference with wild animal populations. Central government involvement is primarily confined to the national parks and reserves and is directed toward the development of Tanzania's tourist potential.[20] Including fisheries and forests as well as wildlife, the entire natural resources budget was allocated only $52 million for the life of the third plan.[21] Even less money was actually spent, making natural resources second only to commerce and tourism as the least-supported sector of the development budget (see Table 2.3). Because of more immediate priorities associated with export crops and general economic recovery, these funding trends show little sign of changing in the later 1980s. Unfortunately, the wildlife situation has not itself stabilized but continues to degenerate steadily.

Four options are open to those seeking wildlife protection, each with its separate implications for human settlement and land use.

1. *Preservation,* the complete insulation of wild animals and their habitats from human interference
2. *Conservation,* limited noneconomic and economic (e.g., commercial hunting) interventions to maintain inferred ecological balances in finite spaces
3. *Utilization,* controlled economic exploitation through devices such as game ranching and moderately to heavily commercialized tourism with its attendant infrastructure
4. Some combination of the above.

Usually expressed in terms of the fourth alternative, these strategies are embodied in regulations and other policies governing the three types of Tanzanian wildlife areas. Game preservation and conservation, together with tourism and a prohibition on settlement, are emphasized in the national parks and game reserves. In the controlled areas, food-oriented game utilization is intended to supplement environmentally safe farming and grazing systems. At ground level, while the scientific, esthetic, and developmental communities debate the relative merits of these preferences, a fifth option has quietly gained support in the controlled areas and near the parks and reserves. This choice features an informal and completely unregulated exploitation of these legally protected ecosystems.

The preservationists stand on one side of the policy debate. Sinclair presents the scientific version of their argument on how best to serve wildlife, his context being Tanzania's largest and most famous national park.

> Systems such as the Serengeti should be maintained in as natural a state as possible to fulfill their functions as National Parks and as ecological baseline areas. Because ecosystems must be considered dynamic, one must resist the temptation to manage them with a view toward maintaining some arbitrary status quo. The present evidence shows that there are natural negative feedback mechanisms operating between some components of the system. Indeed, research must aim at establishing whether feedbacks occur, their nature, and strength of effect. Provided these negative feedbacks are strong enough, the system can absorb disturbances without management.[22]

For their part, conservationists fear that ecological equilibria have been permanently destroyed by human population pressures and increased economic activity, and that the effects of these disturbances are further worsened by enclosing game animals within geographically fixed spaces that cannot support the animals' growing numbers. A joint livestock survey was conducted during the middle 1960s by the United Nations Development Program (UNDP) and the UN Food and Agriculture Organization (FAO). In the words of its final report:

> During the next 20 years it can be anticipated that, with modern techniques of production and marketing, livestock are going to utilize most of the available rangelands of East Africa. The present development plans of the three East African Governments [Kenya, Tanzania, and Uganda] make provision for extensive schemes of land enclosure, water development and improved stock routes and marketing systems. Large ranches owned by development corporations, cooperatives, or individuals are now being developed and many more are planned for the future. Even in Maasailand [which includes the northern Tanzanian parks and reserves], land is now being enclosed and changes in the traditional land tenure system are enabling improved techniques of animal husbandry to be practiced. All such developments are bound to have a serious effect on those wild animal populations, particularly the plains game, which are concentrated in these areas.[23]

2.3   White-bearded gnu, Serengeti National Park. F. Vollmar and World Wildlife Fund.

The UNDP and FAO overestimated the speed and extent of Tanzanian livestock development, but this error does not invalidate the conclusion that human, livestock, and wild animal pressures can easily upset delicate ecological balances. Conservationists maintain that without a development program sensitive to changing animal-habitat interactions, ecological chaos is certain.

Observing that one of Tanzania's greatest health problems is protein-energy deficiency,[24] advocates of wildlife utilization look hopefully to the country's huge herds of wild ungulates and other mammals. Again quoting the UNDP-FAO study:

> Recently published estimates suggest that the Serengeti-Mara region of East Africa (15,000 square miles) contains more than a half million Thomson's gazelle, about a third of a million wildebeest, and 175,000 zebra, in addition to several thousand eland, topis, hartebeest, and elephant. While this represents the most outstanding concentration of plains wildlife in Africa, other areas...still contain a relatively abundant population of wild animals. It has been estimated, for example, that the total weight of wildlife on East Africa's *Acacia* savannas often varies between about 37,000 and 90,000 lb. per square mile, while in the *Acacia-Commiphora* bushlands there are often some 30,000 lb. of wild mammal per square mile. Only rarely are similar weights approached by concentrations of domestic livestock. One of the most important of the many reasons for endeavouring to conserve this wildlife is that it represents a vast potential...source of food for the local population.[25]

The report recommended extensive research and development on wildlife utilization for food and hides. The recommendation has yet to be implemented.

Not unlike its uncertain commitment to tourism, Tanzanian wildlife policies are in a current state of disarray. The game department has also been unable to curb poaching and other forms of encroachment, and wildlife staff are reportedly suffering from low morale and incompetence.[26] More basically, policy choices have not been made that would provide unambiguous performance and funding targets for the wildlife sector. The same must unhappily be said for grass-roots agricultural and rural development.

The Perspective of the Periphery

It has been pointed out that, until very recently at least, agriculture has been assigned a relatively low position in the Tanzanian development budget. So long as peasants remained primarily subsistence producers and were allowed to employ traditional land-use practices, this neglect did not seriously limit their ability to survive in an ecologically balanced manner.[27] Traditional patterns of shifting agriculture offered solutions to problems of soil fertility, wildlife depredation, and insect-borne disease at the level of man-powered peasant technology.

This fact was recognized at a 1979 workshop, jointly sponsored by the University of Dar es Salaam and the International Labor Organization, that closely examined Tanzanian agricultural development policies. "Under the traditional pattern of extensive cultivation, expansion of cultivated areas has been possible without infrastructural investment. The control of the State over access to land is thus much looser than in a land-scarce country of one where new settlement is not possible without heavy infrastructural investment."[28] Conversely, when the state assumes control over access to land, it at once creates a kind of land scarcity and a situation in which public assistance must precede and accompany new settlement. Together with its early emphasis on communalization and its continuing bias in favor of cash-cropping, villagization has transformed rural self-sufficiency into interdependence between the rural areas and the public sector.

At the agricultural periphery, interdependence takes the form of mutually unrequited obligations. From her investigation of village economic activities in Iringa Region, Due concluded that, during the droughts of 1973 and 1974, food yields were consistently higher on cooperative holdings than on communal schemes. She also determined that between 1970 and 1975, per capita food production fell to its 1960 level in both types of settlement.[29] In a study of two communities in the same region, Ndissi found that a lack of technical improvements and investment inputs was more responsible than communalization for low agricultural productivity.[30] Von Freyhold encountered marketing problems that produced similar effects in Tanga Region.[31]

Writing in 1977, Kjekshus described the crisis then facing Tanzanian agricultural systems:

> Unless villagization can be coupled with infrastructural inputs to create a novel technology to master the environment, the nucleated settlement pattern may, by itself, be counter-productive in economic terms and destructive of the ecological balance maintained under the traditional settlement pattern. Nucleated settlement will mean overcrowding of restricted areas with people and domestic animals and the accompanying soil erosion, gully formation and dust-bowls which are all common features in situations where the human initiative has suddenly overtaxed the carrying capacity of the land without compensatory inputs to increase the quality of cultivation. Centralized settlements will mean time wasted in long walks between the new dwellings and the productive fields and will result in the almost certain falling into disuse of the peripheral shambas [farming plots] and their gradual takeover by bush and vermin.[32]

This prediction, which has since materialized in large parts of the country, represents an equal tragedy for wild animals, which are not considered vermin by wildlife advocates. Many grassland species require large open spaces uncontested by dense human populations, and for them a proliferation of overcrowded settlements promises nothing less than extinction.

To confirm these prospects for man and animal, an attempt should be made to narrow the geographical range of analysis. The remainder of this chapter focuses on certain Tanzanian rural areas where the human-wildlife relationship is particularly close and is quickly moving toward a joint struggle for survival.

Wildlife and Land Use in Selected Localities

In an effort to clarify the issues under consideration and to lay a foundation for further research, twenty-one districts in eleven regions were chosen for a study of the wildlife/land-use nexus in modern Tanzania. These administrative units are located in proximity to the country's two great wildlife zones, anchored in the north by the Serengeti National Park and in the south by the vast Selous Game Reserve. Depicted in Figure 2.4, both study areas have experienced serious food shortages since 1973. They are also the scenes of increasing peasant withdrawal into black-market commercial agriculture and nonmarket subsistence cultivation, even in localities where officially marketed cash crops have long been grown. These similarities aside, the area situated north of six degrees latitude differs sharply from the southern study area in terms of food availabilities, population factors, and agricultural system characteristics.

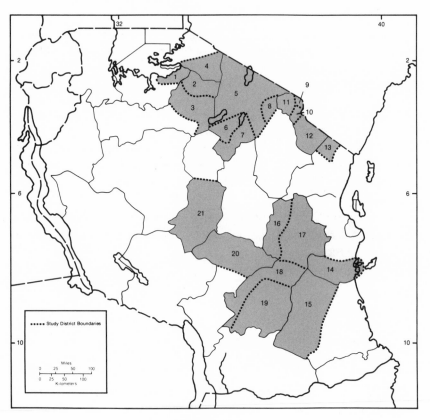

Fig. 2.4. Study Districts

On the basis of the latest available estimates, Table 2.4 suggests that farmers in the northern regions grow a wider variety of staple crops and consume more food calories than their less fortunate southern counterparts. The data further indicate little if any interregional trade in food, except for domestic (supplemented by imported) transfers into heavily urbanized Tanga Region and into Coast Region, which also enjoys easy access to a major port and adjoins the rapidly expanding capital city. Iringa and Singida regions are especially susceptible to food/energy shortages.[33]

Somewhat offsetting these disparities in food availability, the northern group of regions accounts for a larger share of the national population, for a higher average population growth rate, and for an average population density per square kilometer nearly four times that of the other group. Table 2.5 quantifies these distributions as they existed at the time of the last national census. Assuming constant growth rates, the northern population increased by about 1.4 million (from 6.3 to 7.7 mil-

District Names in Figure 2.4	
North	*South*
Mwanza Region	Coast Region
1. Magu	14. Rufiji
Shinyanga Region	Lindi Region
2. Bariadi	15. Liwale
3. Maswa	Morogoro Region
Mara Region	16. Kilosa
4. Serengeti	17. Morogoro Rural
Arusha Region	18. Kilombero
5. Monduli	19. Ulanga/Mahenge
6. Mbulu	Iringa Region
7. Hanang	20. Iringa Rural
8. Arumeru	Singida Region
Kilimanjaro Region	21. Manyoni
9. Rombo	
10. Moshi Rural	
11. Hai	
12. Pare	
Tanga Region	
13. Lushoto	

Table 2.4. Study Region Food Characteristics

Region	Major Staple Crops[a]	Food Production and Availability After Trade and Imports, 1976–1977 (cal/day/capita)	
		Production	Availability
North			
Mwanza	C, R, S	2500–3000	same
Shinyanga	R, S	2500–3000	same
Mara	M, MI, R, S	2000–2500	same
Arusha	M, MI, W	3500–4000	same
Kilimanjaro	B, M, MI, R, W	2000–2500	same
Tanga	B, C, M, R, S	2500–3000	3000–3500
South			
Coast	B, C, R	0000–2000	2000–2500
Lindi	C, R, S	3000–3500	same
Morogoro	B, C, M, R, S	2000–2500	same
Iringa	M, R, W	0000–2000	same
Singida	M, S	0000–2000	same

[a] Bananas (B), Cassava (C), Maize (M), Millet (MI), Rice (R), Sorghum (S), Wheat (W). Locally produced grains contain an average of nine per hundred grams of protein, cassava provides two per hundred grams, and bananas afford only one per hundred grams. Maize and cassava each account for about 24 percent of mainland Tanzania's per capita daily calorie intake, rice for approximately 4 percent; wheat and sorghum for about 3 percent, and millet for slightly more than 2 percent. See Tanzania Ministry of Health, *Tanzania Food Tables* (Nairobi: East African Literature Bureau, 1974), pp. 17, 21, 37; and U.S. Department of Agriculture, *World Food Aid Needs and Availabilities, 1981* (Washington: Economic Research Service, USDA, August 1981), p. 94.

SOURCES: Tanzania Industrial Studies and Consulting Organization, *A Handbook for the Promotion of Industrial Projects* (Dar es Salaam: TISCO, 1980), pp. 41–50; and Tanzania Food and Nutrition Centre, *Data Report on the Food and Nutrition Situation in Tanzania, 1972/73–1976/77* (Dar es Salaam: TFNC, March 1978).

lion) during the seven years between 1978 and 1985, and the southern population grew by approximately 800,000 (from 3.5 to 4.3 million).

District-level population characteristics reflect these regional differences. Concerning the all-important density variable, in 1978 only one northern district ranged below the national average of 19.3 people per square kilometer, while six districts averaged above 75 per square kilometer.[34] In contrast six of eight southern districts averaged below 15 people per square kilometer. Fertility-related factors do not help much in accounting for these variations in density, nor will they in the near future. Seventy-eight percent of northern females and 75 percent of southern females occupied the prospectively and currently most fertile age group in 1978, and the male/female sex ratio was only slightly more than one male per hundred females higher in northern than in southern districts (see Table 2.6). Rather, the environmental agent is most responsible for north-south differences in density. Of greatest importance in this regard is the relationship between rainfall probability and the kinds of agricultural systems that predominate in the north and south.

To understand the ecological ramifications of local population growth and distribution, it is necessary to supplement census data with information on the human carrying capacities of the more and less heavily settled localities. Average annual rainfall probabilities provide acceptable indictors of carrying capacity because, under conditions of relatively unchanged subsistence and cash-crop technologies, rainfall remains the most critical factor in agricultural production.

Table 2.7 estimates rainfall probabilities for the agricultural systems of northern and southern study districts. Except in some of the highlands, which also contain unusually fertile and less easily leached soils, the Tanzanian monsoon rains are often excessively heavy or sparse. Even in "normal" years, only one-third of the country enjoys a 95 percent or better chance of receiving at least 750 millimeters (30 inches) of precipitation, an amount considered necessary for consistently productive cultivation. Another third can expect less than a 85 percent chance of obtaining 500 millimeters (20 inches). At the same time, heavy downpours and flash floods are common throughout much of the country. Two-thirds of Tanzania is frequently too dry or too wet for high crop yields.

These constraints are present in the study areas. Parts of six southern districts receive less than 500 millimeters of rain during the wettest

Table 2.5. Study Region Population Growth and Distribution

Region	1978 Population (percent mainland total)		Average Annual Growth Rate, 1967–1978 (mainland average = 3.3)		Average Density per km², 1978 (mainland average = 19.3)	
			North			
Mwanza	8.4			2.9		73.3
Shinyanga	7.7			3.6		26.1
Mara	4.2			2.6		33.2
Arusha	5.4			3.9		11.3
Kilimanjaro	5.2			3.0		68.1
Tanga	6.0			2.7		38.9
	36.9	Total	Average	3.1	Average	48.1
			South			
Coast	3.0			1.7		15.9
Lindi	3.0			2.1		8.0
Morogoro	5.5			2.9		13.3
Iringa	5.4			2.7		16.2
Singida	3.6			2.7		12.4
	20.5	Total	Average	2.4	Average	13.2

SOURCE: Tanzania, *1978 Population Census Preliminary Report* (Dar es Salaam: Bureau of Statistics, Ministry of Finance and Planning, n.d.), p. 177.

Table 2.6. Study District Population Characteristics, 1978

District	Males	Females	Total	Average Density (km²)	Females 0–34 Years	Percent All Females	M/F Sex Ratio (M per 100 F)
North							
Magu	128,162	130,618	258,780	75.0–99.9	102,508	78.5	99.5
Bariadi	143,029	153,906	296,935	15.0–29.9	106,725	69.3	92.9
Maswa	148,994	154,973	303,967	15.0–29.9	123,324	79.6	96.1
Serengeti	99,629	108,046	207,675	15.0–29.9	83,549	77.3	92.2
Monduli	60,048	58,708	118,756	0.0–14.9	46,725	79.6	102.3
Mbulu	98,552	95,223	193,775	15.0–29.9	76,467	80.3	103.5
Hanang	116,862	114,430	231,292	15.0–29.9	89,626	78.3	102.1
Arumeru	119,383	118,637	238,020	100+	95,428	80.4	100.6
Rombo	74,637	83,102	157,739	100+	64,869	78.1	89.8
Moshi Rural	149,114	162,837	311,951	100+	124,652	76.6	91.6
Hai	86,326	85,991	172,317	75.0–99.9	67,796	78.8	100.4
Pare	101,379	106,785	208,164	15.0–29.9	82,917	77.6	95.0
Lushoto	133,541	152,528	286,069	75.0–99.9	121,178	79.4	87.6
South							
Rufiji	64,043	71,291	135,334	0.0–14.9	47,549	66.7	89.1
Liwale	18,895	20,511	39,406	0.0–14.9	15,471,	75.4	92.1
Kilosa	139,821	134,657	274,478	15.0–29.9	104,513	77.6	103.8
Morogoro Rural	170,046	174,035	344,081	15.0–29.9	128,831	74.0	97.7
Kilombero	67,730	65,277	133,007	0.0–14.9	50,595	77.5	103.8
Ulanga/Mahenge	54,286	59,224	113,510	0.0–14.9	44,478	75.1	91.6
Iringa Rural	130,776	152,325,	290,101	0.0–14.9	121,401	79.7	90.4
Manyoni	49,376	53,027	102,403	0.0–14.9	37,947	71.6	93.1

SOURCE: Tanzania, *1978 Population Census Preliminary Report* (Dar es Salaam: Bureau of Statistics, Ministry of Finance and Planning, n.d.), passim.

part of the year. Those that receive more are typically mountainous and lowland regions prone to soil erosion and flooding. The north displays a more consistent and somewhat drier climate, with the extremes of annual precipitation confined to three of thirteen districts.

Table 2.7. Study District Rainfall and Agricultural Patterns

District	Predominate Annual Rainfall Probabilities[a]	Predominate Agricultural Systems[b]
	North	
Magu	A	1, 2
Bariadi	A, B	1, 2, 3
Maswa	B	1, 2, 3
Serengeti	A	1, 2
Monduli	B	4
Mbulu	B	1, 2, 4
Hanang	B	1, 2, 4
Arumeru	B, C	1, 2, 4
Rombo	C	1, 2, 5
Moshi Rural	B, C	1, 2
Hai	C, D	1, 2, 5
Pare	B	1, 2, 5
Lushoto	A, B, C	1, 2, 5
	South	
Rufiji	A, C, D	1
Liwale	A	6
Kilosa	A, C, D	1, 6
Morogoro Rural	A, C, D	1, 5
Kilombero	D	1, 3
Ulanga/Mahenge	A, C	6
Iringa Rural	A, B, C, D	1, 3, 6
Manyoni	B	6

[a]Less than an 85 percent chance of 500 millimeters in October-May (A); less than an 85 percent chance of 750 millimeters (B); an 85–95 percent chance of 750 millimeters (C); better than a 95 percent chance of 750 millimeters (D).

[b]Intensive smallholder subsistence cultivation (1); an important cattle component in cultivated areas (2); large-scale market cultivation (3); nomadic pastoralism (4); smallholder market cultivation (5); extensive smallholder subsistence cultivation (6).

SOURCES: For rainfall probabilities (see also Figure 2.2), Allison Butler Herrick et al., *Area Handbook for Tanzania* (Washington: U.S. Government Printing Office, 1968), p. 15; for agricultural systems, Clark University Cartographics and Program for International Development, Worchester MA.

Ecological difficulties become apparent for both northern and southern areas when their agricultural systems are considered. Smallholder subsistence cultivation is intensively practiced in virtually all districts. Made possible by rich volcanic soils and generally moderate rainfall, smallholder market agriculture is an important component in Rombo and Hai and in parts of Pare and Lushoto districts. Despite villagization, however, dry weather and poor soils necessitate land-extensive shifting cultivation in five of eight southern districts. By comparing average population densities with rainfall probabilities and agricultural system preferences, it can be hypothesized that northern and southern districts face imminent but different land-use problems.

The main impediment in the north is overcrowding in an environment either too marginal for this level of settlement or so attractive as to have prompted rural concentrations of up to more than 100 people per square kilometer. If the hypothesis is correct, portions of six districts (Magu, Bariadi, Maswa, Serengeti, Mbulu, and Hanang) fall into the first category, two districts (Rombo and Hai) occupy the second, and four districts (Arumeru, Moshi Rural, Pare, and Lushoto) encompass both. Although less affected by density-related land shortages, southern peasants face the equally demanding challenges of shifting agriculture in an environmentally impoverished setting. The hypothesis for them is that scattered pockets of rural overcrowding will be found in the more arable parts of each southern district. With the agricultural technologies now in place, and at present levels of population growth, both north and south may soon confront a terminal shortage of farming and grazing land.

With ominous implications for the people involved, the two propositions are supported by the study districts' rural settlement patterns and land-use strategies. One consequence of these disorders is that wildlife are likewise included in Tanzania's dialectic of population density, land scarcity, and environmental degradation.

THE SETTLEMENT FACTOR

A major goal of the villagization program was to facilitate collective methods of farm production and income distribution, thus making each village "capable of promoting rural development without excessive differentiation in wealth, income, and power."[35] This objective, with its

2.4 Land-intensive agriculture in the north: coffee production in Kilimanjaro Region. Tanzanian Ministry of Agriculture.

2.5   Land-extensive agriculture in the south: Peanut harvesting in Songea Region. Tanzanian Ministry of Agriculture.

promise of socioeconomic and political harmony, is far from being reached.

By 1978, over 90 percent of Tanzania's rural population was settled into about eight thousand officially recognized villages. Of 2.9 million nonurban households, 2.8 million were located in villages and all but 140,000 of these were in registered villages.[36] To be registered, a community must normally contain 250 or more families living together within formally defined boundaries that enclose the village and its surrounding fields. According to law, a village council assigns each family a minimum, one-acre homestead plot and a portion of the surrounding land, the size of which is determined by the family's ability to develop and work it.[37] Livestock remain in private hands, enabling them to be less equally distributed than land holdings.

As shown in Table 2.8, northern and southern study districts share this heavy national commitment to village residence. Two aspects of villagization exercised the greatest initial influence over the study areas.

Table 2.8. Study Region and District Settlement Characteristics, 1978

Region District	Registered Villages	Nonregistered Villages	Dispersed Settlements	Rural Areas	Urban Areas	Total Households	Percent in Villages
			Households in				
			North				
Mwanza	197,545	6,105	3,160	206,810	34,153	240,963	84.5
Magu	39,663	609	25	40,297	1,158	41,455	97.1
Shinyanga	195,825	12,252	5,457	213,534	12,839	226,373	91.9
Bariadi	41,523	178	721	42,422	1,306	43,728	95.4
Maswa	45,079	1,478	781	47,338	2,728	50,066	93.0
Mara	100,817	2,897	2,389	106,103	10,725	116,828	88.8
Serengeti	30,762	1,499	576	32,837	2,446	35,283	91.4
Arusha	120,002	21,377	15,621	157,000	18,721	175,721	80.5
Monduli	9,477	5,639	3,425	18,541	575	19,116	79.1
Mbulu	21,261	8,055	2,911	32,227	748	32,975	88.9
Hanang	38,418	949	3,327	42,694	1,821	44,515	88.4
Arumeru	39,458	2,424	4,060	45,942	0	45,942	91.2
Kilimanjaro	139,940	10,093	2,893	152,926	16,585	169,511	88.5
Rombo	26,941	723	48	27,712	690	28,402	97.4
Moshi Rural	48,825	7,743	373	56,941	0	56,941	99.3
Hai	29,126	0	2,425	31,551	1,470	33,021	88.2
Pare	35,048	1,627	47	36,722	1,089	37,811	97.0
Tanga	157,832	5,801	18,268	181,901	34,238	216,139	75.7
Lushoto	51,265	695	715	52,675	610	53,285	97.5

South

Coast	96,437	9,308	5,707	111,452	8,067	119,519	88.5
Rufigi	28,325	450	1,715	30,490	1,259	31,749	90.6
Lindi	105,847	0	538	106,385	11,688	118,073	89.6
Liwale	5,916	0	23	5,939	1,291	7,230	81.8
Morogoro	140,356	20,322	12,930	173,608	28,517	202,125	79.5
Kilosa	42,857	4,164	5,743	52,764	8,468	61,232	76.8
Morogoro Rural	60,042	10,497	4,266	74,805	985	75,790	93.1
Kilombero	20,280	1,398	2,543	24,221	3,123	27,344	79.3
Ulanga/ Mahenge	17,177	1,236	378	18,791	681	19,472	94.6
Iringa	178,552	2,683	2,790	184,025	18,248	202,273	89.6
Iringa Rural	56,218	0	633	56,851	0	56,851	98.9
Singida	112,426	1,591	5,476	119,493	12,877	132,370	86.1
Manyoni	19,471	0	105	19,576	3,754	23,330	83.5

Source: Tanzania, *1978 Population Census Preliminary Report*. (Dar es Salaam: Bureau of Statistics, Ministry of Finance and Planning, n.d.), pp. 171–173.

These elements have to do with the manner in which village formation has affected subsequent land use. They involve village occupancy rates of less arable and more arable districts and, more importantly, distinctions among villages as to the positioning of households in relation to production fields and grazing areas.

All twenty-one districts are heavily villagized in the official parlance. It should be noted, however, that the term "village" carries different meanings in different places. Where communities were previously dispersed in response to unfavorable environmental conditions, people have now been moved into concentrated settlements and left to farm the outlying land. In more arable cash-crop locations, already proximate homesteads were frequently classified as villages on the basis of contiguous farm holdings. Here the farmers remain close their permanently or semipermanently cultivated fields. A mixed approach was employed among pastoral societies, with cattle-keeping farm communities grouped into villages and seminomads allowed to maintain their nucleated but seasonally mobile camps.

The convenience of creating villages by classification rather than by physical relocation helps explain why cash-crop districts seem more completely villagized than districts predominately or totally devoted to subsistence agriculture. Seven of the ten study districts with the highest percentage of village households (Maswa, Morogoro Rural, Bariadi, Pare, Rombo, Lushoto, and Iringa Rural) are also committed to market cultivation, and only one of the eleven least villagized districts (Hai) is likewise engaged. In short, villagization exerted little direct impact on land use in cash-crop areas, already densely settled before the campaign was launched. The same cannot be said about localities where environmental conditions had led to low-density settlement patterns in which long-fallow shifting cultivation could be practiced. These areas became the primary targets of the resettlement authorities.

It has been pointed out that two techniques were traditionally used to overcome problems of rural overcrowding. In the fruitful highlands and in other locations of limited space but high potential, the answer lay in an intensification of production and the introduction of measures to maintain soil fertility and prevent erosion. A less complicated procedure was selected in most of Tanzania, however, that of simply moving on to new land.

Lele described the latter course of action in Sukumaland, located in

Mwanza and Shinyanga regions. The colonial government's tsetse fly eradication projects and a gradual reduction of intra-ethnic tensions among the Sukuma opened previously uninhabited territory to humans and livestock and encouraged the demographically expanding Sukuma to claim it. As a result, the average Sukuma farm holding remained of fairly constant size between 1948–1950 and 1967–1970, while the population increased at an average annual rate of between 1.3 and 1.5 percent in the traditionally settled areas and between 3.2 and 5.4 percent in the newly opened frontier locations. Lule also reported that, from 1955 to 1970, farmers in the more recently settled areas were able to raise their cotton output by 346 percent, as opposed to a 113 percent increase in Sukumaland's older cotton-producing regions.[38]

By consolidating peripheral rural populations and by freezing mobility, villagization seriously compromised this reaction to land shortages. Instead, the policy has created several problems for the Sukuma and for other societies facing similar pressures. Among these difficulties are less readily available land, growing socioeconomic inequality, and environmental destruction that can occur with astonishing speed.

Members of the workshop sponsored by the University of Dar es Salaam and the ILO observed the first two dilemmas on a field trip to Chekereni Village in Kilimanjaro Region, where a large number of peasants had not been allocated homestead plots because of insufficient village land. The group discovered that some farmers were forced to walk long distances to cultivate plots they still owned elsewhere. It was also determined that about 30 percent of the village's production land was under dispute with neighboring settlements.[39] Inequalities were perpetuated at Chekereni, and perhaps made even greater—inequalities that villagization was designed to overcome. These disparities were of the sort van Hekken and van Velzen had noticed earlier in Rungwe District of southern Mbeya Region. Here "certain groups among the peasantry do not have sufficient access to land to cover their daily needs in terms of subsistence requirements" because "the fields which guarantee a markedly higher yield per man day or allow for the cultivation of marketable or other valuable crops are in the hands of a minority."[40]

From the standpoint of wildlife protection, socioeconomic imbalances of this nature provide incentives to poach and to encroach upon game lands. Equally worrisome are the short-term environmental effects of villagization. In his study of Mbozi District in western Mbeya, Knight observed a phenomenon that has by now become common enough to attract considerable foreign press attention.[41] "If the population density exceeds the critical value [of what long-fallow cultivation can support], the fallow must be shortened. But, having shortened the fallow, land is then less productive and the area of cultivation in any one year must increase, which means a further shortening of the fallow. Hence a spiral results that seemingly ends in disaster."[42] Since Knight wrote these comments, villagization has worsened the situation by removing what mobility peasant farmers were able to muster, converting their reduced-fallow alternative into a zero-fallow acceleration of soil depletion. The only legally sanctioned recourse to overpopulation and complete soil exhaustion is to form new villages, thereby further spreading the damage.[43] Because wildlife have mostly been limited to agriculturally poor environments, this dynamic is sure to have a devastating impact on them.

Writing in 1977 before the consequences of villagization and the magnitude of recent population growth were better understood, Nieuwolt classified five of the present study districts and isolated parts of seven others as overpopulated for their rainfall capacities. He designated only one district as underpopulated and the remainder as able to accommodate their populations.[44] The following observations and concluding case-study examples suggest that villagization, stagnated agricultural development, and unabated population growth have since placed portions of all twenty-one districts into the overpopulated category, with the expected outcomes for their human inhabitants and for the wild animals that exist near them.

THE CRISIS IN CARRYING CAPACITY

Steeped in the paternalism of its time, the colonial handbook for mainland Tanzania summarized the traditional attitudes of rural dwellers toward wildlife as follows: "The average African regards game from a purely realistic point of view. In his opinion, it is something which invades his plantations, kills his stock (and occasionally himself), which was created to be eaten and, latterly, which is a certain source of income."[45] To these perceptions of game animals as pests, food, and profit must today be added one other—that of wildlife as dangerous rivals in a climactic struggle for the *pori*, the still unexploited bush, forests, and grasslands. From the peasant perspective, expanding the agricultural commons is the most critical issue, and its immediacy is far greater than the need for technical and economic assistance enabling peasants to produce more on less land. In one perceptive observation, "the point at issue is much deeper than the well-documented exclusion of the poor from credit, extension and marketing services. For, from the point of view of the poor, it is less a matter of exclusion from potential sources of increased productivity than a matter of being deprived of productive resources that they already own or control. The most central of these resources is land."[46] Tanzanian peasants may not yet control the country's game land, but because of their increasingly desperate circumstances, they are inexorably being driven to claim it as their own.

Until population growth and villagization upset the fragile land-use balances of both areas, northern and southern study districts displayed differences in population pressure resembling those Shrestha discovered in rural Nepal. He found that locations of high population density were not necessarily overpopulated and, in fact, were frequently underpopulated for their agricultural carrying capacities. Population pressures seemed greatest in agriculturally marginal places, where low densities belied high ratios of population to cultivated land.[47] As occurred in Nepal, farmers in the more densely populated districts of northern Tanzania reduced their demographic stresses by intensifying and coordinating cash and food crop production. Environmentally deprived of this solution, shifting cultivators and pastoralists in the lightly settled northern and southern districts controlled their population densities by dispersing into unsettled areas. Innovative husbandry, improved nutrition, and higher economic returns led to further population growth and to yet greater densities and agricultural carrying capacities in the more arable northern districts.[48]

Both of these environmentally sensitive land-use strategies were followed in accordance with a decision rule, formally posited by Chisholm, that smallholders tend everywhere to adopt:

> It is an observed fact that in agriculture each successive dose of inputs—say hours of work—tends to yield a smaller and smaller return as the total amount of inputs—the total number of hours worked—rises. Hence the farmer will desist at a point earlier on the curve of diminishing returns the more each actual hour of work applied to the land costs; which is to say, the further away is the field.[49]

Combined with relatively slow population growth, with tsetse infestations in potential livestock regions, and with the enforced depopulation of national parks and game reserves, this modus operandi kept rural dwellers close to their best holdings. In this way, not only were the parks and reserves protected, but also the game controlled areas in which settlement is permitted.

But as Ruthenberg noted in the middle 1960s, postindependence population growth radically destabilized Tanzanian farming systems.[50] The lightly peopled northern and southern study districts experienced rapid expansion of cultivation and grazing, and farmers in the densely settled northern districts further intensified their cash and food crop production in an attempt to maintain yields on steadily shrinking plots. Ruthenberg pointed out then that these adjustments were leading to their own points of diminishing returns. Even before villagization worsened the situation, he warned of an imminent stagnation or decline in farm output and incomes. Beginning in easily exhausted areas like Sukumaland and the Usambara Mountains of Lushoto District, technologically unaccommodated land shortages quickly lowered the marginal returns of both land and labor.

> The smaller the holding the lower is the average gross return and the marginal gross return per acre, simply because the smaller the holding the smaller is the scope for cash production with crops yielding high returns per acre. The smaller smallholdings are consequently, due to the priority attached to subsistence food production, caught in a situation which might well be designated as a "low level equilibrium trap." The only way out—except for migrating—is to attain increasing returns per acre of a given crop by constantly improving husbandry, and there are hardly any indications that this is being done.[51]

Among its other goals, villagization sought to enhance cash-cropping by substituting a more efficient mobilization of labor for scarce financial and managerial resources. This choice paralleled a line of thinking that apparently motivated the communalization of agriculture in China.[52] Lacking the organizational and coercive aspects of Chinese communalization, however, villagization only exacerbated an already serious decline in agricultural production. The program also intensified both rural and urban population concentrations by encouraging rural-to-urban as well as rural-to-rural migration. But, as Monsted and Walji observed, the migrants remaining in the rural areas are less likely to make productive improvements than are the younger, better-educated, and more entrepreneurial people who move to the cities.[53]

Population growth, externally unassisted resettlement, and grassroots attitudinal conservatism have combined to reduce agricultural carrying capacities in each of the study districts. Although considerably more research is needed on the subject, these processes can be sketched in relation to their impact on Tanzania's two largest wildlife complexes. The analysis here concludes with these reflections.

LAND USE AND NORTHERN WILDLIFE AREAS

The most pressing ecological problem in the northern Tanzanian districts involves unmitigated human and livestock pressures on the available land. In both the northeast and the northwest, consistent population growth has led to increasing fragmentation of farm holdings, to more numerous legal conflicts over land-use rights, to environmentally destructive reductions of fallow periods, and to the propagation of hardier but nutritionally less adequate food crops as agriculturally inferior areas are brought under cultivation. Although livestock are individually owned, grazing land is typically treated as a pastoral commons. The constant addition of livestock has resulted in overstocking and overgrazing and an ever-increasing number of emaciated animals. These difficulties are not entirely new and in some cases extend well back into the colonial period.

In the Usambara Mountains to the south of the Mkomazi Game Reserve, Attems witnessed an agrarian "involution" that by 1965 had created worse economic conditions than before colonial development efforts began seventy years earlier.[54] In this southernmost part of Lushoto District, a rapidly growing but topographically limited Shambala society was forced to convert its shifting cultivation into permanent cropping with up to three harvests per year. Consequently, family subsistence plots and communal grazing areas became smaller and more widely scattered, erosion off the steep slopes lowered soil fertility, cassava replaced maize and beans as the chief staple, and the once-thriving Shambala cattle became more and more undernourished. The Shambala's reluctance to apply labor-intensive techniques to improve soil fertility (such as terracing and ridging, manuring, and weeding) and the failure of official extension services to persuade them in this direction served to transform a formerly self-supporting locality into one of "considerable pauperization...which, if allowed to continue, will result in one of the most impoverished smallholder economies to be found in East Africa."[55]

Already compelled to live in concentrated settlements and to walk long distances to their widely scattered fields, the Shambala were merely sustained in their involution by the villagization policy. The only land left for them now to occupy lies in the arid northern reaches of Lushoto District, that is, in the Mkomazi Game Reserve.

The situation is somewhat less critical in Kilimanjaro Region, but perhaps not for long. Kilimanjaro also includes the Mkomazi reserve as well as the Kilimanjaro National Park, and it adjoins the Arusha National Park in Arusha Region. Beginning in the 1920s, population pressure and an increasing commercialization of agriculture induced the Chagga people of Hai, Rombo, and Moshi Rural districts to open new land for cultivation, to farm more intensively, and increasingly to engage in socially disintegrative litigations over land rights. Population pressure has also brought about more recent Chagga migrations into farming locations beyond their home districts, has prompted the younger and better-educated to seek urban employment, and has caused all segments of the society to experience growing unemployment and underemployment.

Hai, Rombo, and Moshi Rural absorbed an estimated 35 percent population increase between 1967 and 1978, creating rural densities exceeding three hundred people per square kilometer in some places. Traditional farming areas are constrained since rich volcanic soils and 2,000-millimeter (80-inch) annual rainfall are limited to the slopes of Mt. Kilimanjaro. Chagga soil conservation and intercropping adaptations have not enabled more people to be accommodated in the highlands, and the society has been forced to expand into the lowland zone with its shallow soils and annual rainfall of less than 800 millimeters (32 inches).

In his detailed study of Chagga agricultural practices between 1920 and 1970, Maro confirmed Boserup's hypothesis that population growth will prompt a successful intensification of cultivation under favorable environmental conditions.[56] He also found that higher incomes resulting from the combined output of bananas, coffee, and livestock encouraged population growth and land scarcity, which contributed to a further diversification into dairying and cardamon cultivation and to another cycle of population growth and land shortage. Writing in 1974 when Chagga out-migration was gaining momentum, Maro concluded that "as a limit on agricultural productivity is reached, the Wachagga will have either to migrate to other parts of the country or to find non-agricultural ways of earning a living if a balance between resources and population is to be maintained."[57] With the slopes of Kilimanjaro either fully occupied or claimed by the Kilimanjaro National Park, and with wage employment in a present state of decline,[58] it may be that most Chagga will soon confront the one alternative that has compelled some to migrate as far away as Mozambique—to move into progressively less inviting areas and there to disrupt the indigenous ecosystems. The inevitable damage will be accelerated if these outcasts are required to live in villages that for all practical purposes remain unassisted.

A similar dilemma faces the Sukuma, Maasai, and other societies of northwestern Tanzania. In the Sukuma districts of Mwanza and Shinyanga regions, cotton production was dramatically increased following World War II. As noted earlier, this growth in output (from 6,000 tons in 1947 to 41,000 tons in 1962–1964) did not result from improved husbandry of the land. Rather, it was brought about by shortening the fallow periods, by mobilizing the grazing commons for cultivation, and by opening virgin bushlands in Sukuma expansion areas. Even then, outmigration threatened the Maswa Game Reserve and the western Serengeti and was reinforced by unprecedented population increases in postwar Sukumaland.[59]

Like other peasant societies, the Sukuma were lured by economic rewards and then forced by population growth into practicing intensive agriculture with the technologies of shifting cultivation. As von Rhotenhan concluded in 1963, this incongruence was accentuated by the sort of attitudinal conservatism that Monsted and Walji have generally attributed to rural-rural migrants:

> The reason why a large majority of the Wasukuma sticks to the traditional methods and is not prepared to take advantage of improvement which would lead to steadily rising yields per acre is probably to be sought in the time-lag between the level of economic development and inherited attitudes. Although semi-permanent cultivation is practiced on half-commercialized farms, an attitude of mind is still prevalent which stems largely from the time of shifting cultivation.[60]

Von Rhotenhan predicted that as the remaining virgin territories fell under cultivation and their soils became exhausted, Sukuma cultivators would either suffer greatly diminished productivity or be induced to improve their agricultural practices with innovations such as regular weeding, fertilization, mechanization, and irrigation. He added, however, that "the individual farmer can do little, unless administrative services and actions create the institutional base on which he can develop his holding."[61] One of the most villagized and land-hungry people of Tanzania, the Sukuma have yet to receive this assistance.

Population growth, density, and rural migration have affected not only the Sukuma's cropping systems but also their livestock economy and that of neighboring local societies. Von Rhotenhan noted considerable overgrazing on the shrinking pastoral commons of Sukumaland, where no traditional limits were placed on the total number of cattle. In his own study of overgrazing, pasture deterioration, and soil erosion, Mackenzie ascribed these problems not so much to a lack of land capacity as to inadequate pasture management. Limited in their expansion by

2.6　Opening the savannah: field preparation near Wawani Village, Arusha Region. Tanzanian Ministry of Agriculture.

the protected wildlife areas and not having access to sufficient range-management inputs and reliable sources of water, the Sukuma and other groups have resorted to an age-old contingency plan—to accumulate as many cattle as possible in wet years so that some will survive during dry periods.[62] Pastoral societies, prominently the Maasai, also burn their ranges to provide for lush wet-season pastures. This custom destroys dry-season forages, leads to the disappearance of perennial grasses and to their replacement by fire-resistant but less nutritious plant species, and causes excessive water run-off and soil erosion during the rainy season.[63] The study districts located in Mwanza, Shinyanga, Mara, and Arusha regions lie in the heart of the eastern African cattle complex and contain a large share of Tanzania's national herd. In its major study of the complex, the 1960's UN research team drew the following conclusions about the grazing commons of Sukumaland:

> At present there are few signs that the customary attitudes to land tenure are likely to change. This is understandable, because a satisfactory alternative to the present system has not yet shown itself. An enclosure movement based on individual holdings is likely to create serious inequities in land distribution and would certainly be resisted strongly by the people; it would present problems of access to watering points and hedges would utilize unproductively a considerable area of land in the aggregate. Basic to the whole problem is the fact that in most areas of Sukumaland there are too many people on too little land. It seems that the most promising line would be to base reform on village units, so that groups of people would have joint jurisdiction over the local grazing rights and would jointly operate local schemes of pasture and animal husbandry. But any moves to reform systems of land tenure in settled areas of Sukumaland must be accompanied by well-organized schemes of land settlement in adjacent unoccupied areas.[64]

Although the villages have been created, these types of land reform and livestock development remain goals rather than realities in the densely populated areas and at the quickly filling periphery of human settlement.

In the periphery, at the point of physical contact among pastoralists, pioneering cultivators, and wildlife, the land-use problem is exacerbated by diseases such as trypanosomiasis and rinderpest. O'Conner describes the effects:

Animals as well as insects may assist in the spread of disease. The tsetse fly not only depends on certain types of vegetation for its habitat, but also relies on wild animals for most of its food, carrying trypanosomiasis from one such animal to another and ultimately to cattle. Tsetse eradication methods have therefore included the destruction of game as well as of bush. In this way the presence of cattle is often related to the absence of game. These measures of course conflict with efforts toward game conservation, and the result is increased regional differentiation, with an increase of wild animals in some areas and a decrease in others.[65]

This phenomenon has been detected in the Serengeti, where human and livestock migrations from Magu, Bariadi, and Serengeti districts have helped increase central and western populations of the parks' large ungulates.[66] But it cannot be assumed that movements of pastoralists and cultivators will eventually stop at the Serenegeti boundaries, any more than that these invisible frontiers have prevented an epidemic of poaching in the park. In fact, what has been praised as "one of the few remaining vestiges of a naturally operating grazing system"[67] for large ungulates may well become their graveyard as they are compressed into ever-smaller spaces. The same can be said for these and other species in all the northern game areas, upon which (one might add) Tanzania's fledgling tourist industry depends.

LAND USE AND SOUTHERN WILDLIFE AREAS

The workshop sponsored by the University Dar es Salaam and the ILO in 1979 concentrated on rural development in northern Tanzania. From the field observations of its members, the workshop recommended that "in the medium to long run, incentives to settle elsewhere in land abundant parts of the country must play a major role in relieving land shortage."[68] This proposal implies two unanswered questions. Will the incentives to resettle come in the form of technical and economic assistance for those involved in this exodus, or will they remain the negative stimuli of inadequate development assistance, overpopulation, and declining subsistence yields? Moreover, will such extensive movements of people transcend the geographical limits of past rural-to-rural migrations? If far-flung relocations do occur, they may feature innovatively unsophisticated northern peasants moving into sparsely settled southern districts.[69] But under current productive circumstances, numerous limitations insure that large parts of the south are lightly populated, and some of these factors also help explain why huge tracts in southern Tanzania are taken up by national parks and game reserves.

In the Kilombero River valley of northern Kilombero District, the indigenous Pogoro people traditionally lived near the banks of the river and cultivated dry-season rice as their main staple crop. When the Selous Game Reserve was established by the colonial authorities, most of these people were moved to higher ground where dry-season rice could not be grown. When the Selous was later expanded to its present size of 55,000 square kilometers (22,000 square miles), more and more households moved westward to the vicinity of the major north-south trunk road. Cassava replaced rice in this less arable part of Kilombero, and short rotations supplanted the long cultivation cycles of the past. Newly settled peasants turned to sugar cane and cotton in an attempt to supplement their incomes with cash, and famine relief food was widely distributed by the government and by local missions when food crops failed. As population densities rose, short-rotation agriculture gave way to semipermanent and permanent cropping; but the peasants still employed agricultural techniques developed for long-fallow rotations of up to forty-five years in the better-watered valley. Cattle were impossible to maintain in the resettlement area because of tsetse infestations, which spread from inside the reserve.[70]

Baum reported that by the middle 1960s, Kilombero's "agricultural take-off" continued to be prevented by a lack of technical innovation, by insect pests and wild animals, and by unpredictable water supplies.[71] Highly capitalized pilot village settlements were instituted to help remove these obstacles, but they proved too expensive to be replicated in sufficient numbers. Baum inferred from the village settlement experiment that "either the settlement management must work with substantial extra [financial] allotments, requiring subsidies, or the incomes of the settlers will be so low that they will not supply the essential incentive needed to secure participation."[72] After Baum left Kilombero, 79 percent of the population was compelled to live in villages, but these "substantial extra allotments" have not been provided.

Even excluding the riverine section claimed by Selous, the Kilombero Valley is not overpopulated for its potential carrying capacity. Table 2.6 indicates that in 1978 the total population of the district was just 133,000, or an average of about ten people per square kilometer. Writing in 1965 when the population was slightly more than 100,000, Jätzold and Baum argued that, in fact, underpopulation posed a more serious impediment to agricultural development: "The population of the Kilombero Valley is probably inadequate, both numerically and qualitatively, to sustain large-scale development schemes on their own. Colonists from outside will therefore have to be brought in."[73] But in another qualitative sense Kilombero *is* overpopulated. Because of their environmentally destructive land-use practices, their enforced village residence, and their lack of outside assistance, Kilombero's peasant communities may have reached the local limits of agricultural carrying capacity. Migrants from other parts of Tanzania must choose between competing with the established inhabitants or settling closer to the Kilombero River by invading the northwestern Selous.

Essentially the same conditions seem to prevail in the remaining southwestern study districts[74] and in the southeast. In southeastern Liwale District, about 40,000 people, mostly of the Ngindo society, were relocated beyond the original boundaries of the Selous.[75] More Ngindo were resettled as the game reserve was expanded, culminating in the mid-1970s with the villagization of eastern Liwale. In his study of Horowe Village in the Matandu River valley, Matzke described a similar evolution of settlement patterns to that which had taken place in Kilombero.

Ethnic warfare, the nineteenth-century slave trade, and the harsh episodes of German colonialism had forced the Ngindo to move closer together in the *miombo* (mixed) woodlands and to relocate into homesteads loosely strung out along the river banks. Now living in closer physical proximity, the Ngindo and their cattle became more susceptible to trypanosome-bearing tsetse flies, which infest the *miombo*. The colonial government attempted a further consolidation of the population so that one- to two-mile-wide strips could be cleared of bush. This action would have disrupted the disease vector by eliminating the habitat of its carrier, but the effort failed because it conflicted with the Ngindo's preference for isolation from government and other ethnic groups, and also with their shifting agricultural practices. An easier solution was adopted of simply abandoning the *miombo* to the Selous, in that way quickly depopulating large areas.[76]

Horowe was formed in 1961 along the banks of the Matandu and was vacated in 1974 when the entire community was transported to a nucleated village some distance from the river. Matzke found that linear river bank settlement had exercised a negative influence on some wild animals in the vicinity, especially on species that prefer the grassy river valleys to the wooded *miombo*. Two months after Horowe was reestablished at its present site, grassland ungulates began returning to the river valley.[77] The concentrated settlement structure of new Horowe has, in turn, produced a low disturbance value for these and other fauna because of its concentration of people in one place and its separation of cultivators from their fields. Although it benefits the resident wildlife, however, Horowe's tightly gathered residential pattern threatens the Ngindo, who must contend with it.

In spite of the man-made and natural hardships of the past, Ngindo farmers developed an agricultural land-use strategy suited to the variable soil quality of Liwale District. Their dispersed and loosely contiguous households permitted a kind of "nomadic" bush-fallow cultivation by offering the greatest possible flexibility in the selection of field sites.[78] The Ngindo lived close by their productive fields, which saved working time and protected crops from marauding animals. When the soil neared exhaustion and the output of plots began to decline, a homestead merely relocated to a different site. Villagization fundamentally disrupted this highly adaptive procedure and tipped the balance in favor of the wildlife by removing peasants from the better riverine soils, from their crops, and from easy access to a permanent water source.

Villages such as Horowe mean less utilization of arable land and quicker depletion of the soil that is farmed, increased travel time to the production plots, and additional crop losses due to wild animal depredations. Unless development assistance is provided or considerable force is used to maintain the villages intact, it is unlikely that villagization in Liwale will escape the fate that overtook the colonial attempt at concentration. As Matzke predicted,

> the Ngindo culture has incorporated a great deal of mobility within it. This mobility will be severely compromised by forced villagization. Since the plans as implemented are static, there is no place for the traditional nomadism of the Ngindo. If their previous experience with closer settlement is any guide, some modification is likely with people returning to a more dispersed linear settlement pattern if it is allowed by the political authorities.[79]

If this dispersal happens, the historical "conflict at the man/wildlife interface" will be renewed and intensified, and population growth will inexorably push the Ngindo back into the Selous.

These and similarly affected peasant farmers fully appreciate the survival value of their traditional land-use customs. They are also coming to recognize the value of the Selous Game Reserve, which they define in precisely the same terms that inspire wildlife advocates. In the words of a former senior game warden, "it is not just a big empty part of the ordinary monotonous *miombo* country that takes up most of southern Tanzania; it's well-watered, it's vast, it's almost entirely surrounded by sparsely populated country, it's an ecological unit."[80] Large expanses are needed for land-extensive agriculture, but populations are becoming less sparse. If agricultural development remains elusive it is only a matter of time before rural dwellers seek to reclaim their niches in this ecosystem and in others like it. As populations and densities continue to grow, these incursions will prove disastrous for humans and animals alike.

Conclusion

It was suggested in Chapter 1 that throughout eastern Africa human and wildlife populations have long interacted in a mutually uncertain quest for survival and dominance. Events in this century have converted simple uncertainty into a crisis of Malthusian proportions for both people and wild animals. Contemporary Tanzanian policy makers have made some attempts to stabilize each side of the man-land-wildlife equation on behalf of income-earning tourism and agricultural development. Lamentably, their actions to protect indigenous species and to rationalize agricultural land use have been meager, ideologically biased, and developmentally dysfunctional. As a result, many of Tanzania's human and nonhuman inhabitants face immediate threats to their existence in the later 1980s and 1990s.

This downward spiral of misery and death can only be reversed through the collective wisdom and concerted efforts of decision makers and administrators in the public sector. For Tanzania to rescue its threatened life forms, the inadequacies of past public policy will have to be replaced by a systematic process of informed goal selection, vigorous policy implementation, and exacting performance evaluation in the country's wildlife and agrarian land-use sectors. Tanzania can no longer afford to entrust its wealth of land and animals to the law of the commons, by which individuals and governments act in their own self-interests and bring disaster to all.

Chapter 4 examines current trends and needed reforms in Tanzanian wildlife and land-use policy. For people, environment, and wildlife, the critical question is whether the necessary transformations will occur in time to render needless the prayer of one Shinyanga farmer:

> Dear God, it is our sins that have destroyed your lovely garden in Shinyanga. Please forgive the man who in his greed keeps 100 cows when 10 would be enough for him and his family. Please forgive the man who cuts down and burns the trees to cultivate new soil after he has ruined the old. Please, God, also forgive the government official who neglects to stop him who doesn't know what he is doing.[81]

—————————— 3 ——————————

Land Use and Wildlife in Modern Kenya

NORMAN N. MILLER

Introduction

Two basic truths underline Kenyan land-use and wildlife realities.[1] First, both policy arenas are highly politicized, not only because of the value Kenyans attach to land ownership and the quick economic returns that can flow from wildlife, but also because land and wildlife have together become the objects of conflicting local, national, and international goals. In short, rural dwellers are determined to defend their farming and grazing areas and to protect themselves, their crops, and their livestock from wild animals. Poachers and other wildlife exploiters treat game animals as obvious and easily accessible sources of profit. National elites look to wildlife-related tourism as a major producer of foreign exchange, which is badly needed both for economic development and for acquiring imported food and luxury consumables for the Kenyan elite class. International visitors and wildlife advocates want to observe and preserve the

3.1 Can both prevail? Lioness at the outskirts of Nairobi in Nairobi National Park: David Keith Jones.

animals, which they prize as irreplaceable esthetic and scientific treasures. Little agreement is ever reached between those who contend with
wildlife on a day-to-day basis and those who wish to protect them for
other purposes.

A second fact is that rural and urban population growth has placed
an increasing premium on the grasslands and other dispersal areas
claimed by humans and wild animals. As food shortages plague the cities
and famines touch the countryside, an unpleasant choice arises between
land and food for human consumption versus land and food for wildlife.
Population pressures as well as competing socioeconomic interests inexorably lead to political dissent. The purpose of this chapter is to examine
both sets of issues in the public policy context of contemporary Kenya.

Wildlife and Kenya's Human Population

The demographic position of Kenya is much the same as Tanzania's, but
at significantly higher levels of population growth and density. Table 3.1
depicts a constant 4 percent average annual growth rate between 1980
and 1983, probably the highest rate of natural increase in the world. The
average density of people per square kilometer rose by nearly 13 percent
during these years. As population growth passes beyond 4 percent to an
estimated 4.4 percent, the 1983 population will double before the end of
the century, and the average density will likewise climb from 32 to 64
people per square kilometer.

Table 3.1. Kenyan Population Growth, 1980–1983

Year	Total Population	Estimated Annual Growth Rate (%)	Average Density (per km²)
1980	16,667,000	-	28.6
1981	17,342,000	4.0	29.8
1982	18,035,000	4.0	31.0
1983[a]	18,748,000	4.0	32.2

[a]Estimated.

SOURCE: Kenya, *Economic Survey 1983* (Nairobi: Central Bureau of Statistics, Ministry of Economic Planning and Development, 1983), p. 10.

As noted earlier in this study, however, only parts of the country are readily farmable under present agricultural conditions, and densities in these central and western highlands soon might range up to many hundreds of Kenyans per square kilometer. Unless agricultural carrying capacities can be improved, the highlands breadbasket will not be able to sustain this mass of rural dwellers, let alone the other centers of growing population pressure—the towns and cities where about 15 percent of the national population resides. Urban communities have swelled at an average annual rate of over 7 percent since the early 1970s, representing an influx exceeded only by Mozambique, Tanzania, and Zaire among low-income African countries.[2]

Untenable circumstances in the rural areas encourage urban migration and help create equally unlivable urban environments. The early effects of increasing rural densities and declining carrying capacities are already becoming apparent in Kenya. Although nearly 80 percent of the labor force is employed in agriculture, the contribution of this sector to the gross domestic product fell from 38 percent before independence to 33 percent by 1982. In each year from 1970 to 1982, total agricultural production suffered an average per capita loss of 1.2 percent and an average 1.9 percent shortfall in the food category.[3] Food shortages are regularly felt among urban refugees from rural overcrowding and also among those who stayed behind and are beginning to spill into lands considered unfit for human settlement barely a decade ago. These places include the 7 percent of Kenya's land area that has been put aside for wildlife.

Population growth generates a demand for land in areas traditionally reserved for game. As a result, cultivation extends into ecologically marginal zones where new farms encroach on game controlled areas. Ultimately, humans and animals clash. Marauding animals destroying crops are shot or speared, particularly if farmers are trying to get established by "clearing the area." High-risk farming and grazing ventures quickly spring up in arid rangelands, where peasants are willing to risk their livestock and to tolerate two or three years of drought in the hope of obtaining one good crop. In these lands, too, humans kill or displace game.

The human tide is also pressing into the wildlife buffer zones, traditional dispersal areas that game move into and out of on a seasonal basis. Around Amboseli Lake, for example, large ungulates are protected during the dry season. When the rains come, these animals migrate toward new grass on the open plains and there confront farmers and herders.

Prohibiting rural dwellers from seeking their livelihood in these expanses or keeping them from killing game on their holdings are very difficult undertakings. When a buffalo, rhino, baboon, hyena, or wild dog threatens a crop or a child, the community's consensus is to eliminate the animal. That a poor man can make a year's earnings by dispatching a leopard or a lion and five years' wages by killing a rhino seems a compelling economic incentive. Against these perceived necessities and enticements, government is often helpless.

Ian Parker, a wildlife writer and researcher, emphasizes that the rapid proliferation of Kenya's human population is the central issue in wildlife survival.

> The density problem is at the core of the issue. If you increase the density of people, there is no possible way animals can survive, particularly if the people are poor and rural, which of course they are in Kenya. The population explosion is the main strand in the rope that is hanging wildlife, and the process can be predicted with some accuracy. Again, it involves the relationship between civic laws and game laws, the human population and the animal population. . . . As human density increases, laws will become more stringent. Population pressures will force rural people to break the laws more frequently, causing a great deal of social and political unrest, to the point that the government will in all likelihood have to back down from greater enforcement. Kenya will never go to extreme measures to maintain the game. At some point the system must crash. The animal population will decline so much the laws will become meaningless and thus will either be rescinded, revoked, or ignored. In essence, human population growth will cause greater game regulations and restrictions for a time, but this will not protect the wildlife, and the animals will decline—in number, in species, in biomass, in density—however you want to measure it.[4]

Illustrated in Figure 3.1, this scenario poses a Malthusian prospect for wildlife analogous to that proposed in the last chapter for the Tanzanian human society. This outcome may ultimately overtake both countries' wildlife populations and may be played out at an even faster rate than in Tanzania despite Tanzania's weaker counterforce of wildlife advocacy. The remainder of this discussion is devoted to an analysis of the various factors at work in the Kenyan version of the process, factors that are acting to hasten or retard its completion at point "Y"—high human population, low or no animal population, and no enforceable laws.

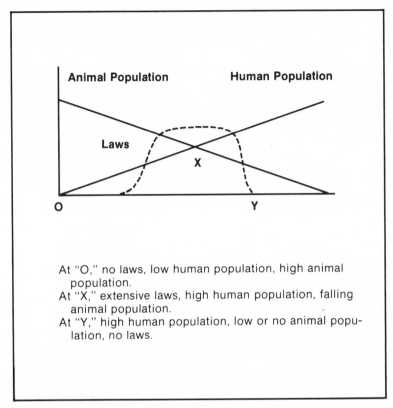

At "O," no laws, low human population, high animal population.
At "X," extensive laws, high human population, falling animal population.
At "Y," high human population, low or no animal population, no laws.

Fig. 3.1. Population and Regulation

Economic and Equity Factors

Questions of equity immediately complicate the land-use and wildlife issues. The economic rationale that "game must pay its way" has been advanced as the prime reason for saving wildlife. By balancing human and animal needs, it is argued, wildlife can earn their keep. This goal, according to most ecologists, requires game cropping, particularly of wildebeest, zebra, and buffalo, and a systematic method of paying landowners on whose domains animals are shot. If properly controlled, this practice would provide expanding local communities with income, make game animals valuable to them, and provide them with incentives to conserve the animals and their habitats. It would also enhance official revenues through licences, taxes, and tourist earnings.

Although more seriously attempted than in Tanzania, efforts to persuade rural Kenyans of the value of wildlife have been unsuccessful for several reasons. First, until recently no one had even proposed arrangements under which game and other wildlife could acquire legitimate economic meaning to Africans living in proximity to large clusters of wild fauna. The government's standard position, that wildlife are simply "state property," only breeds dissent and disobedience. The international conservationists' suggestion that Kenyans bear a moral obligation to preserve wildlife as a "heritage for mankind" appears highly irrelevant to the rural poor. Educational approaches and extension efforts that rest on a "you should and therefore you shall" rationale merely fall on deaf ears.

A formal campaign during the 1960s to introduce Western conservation values to Kenya quickly became a documented failure. Karen Carlson pointed out in her detailed study that wildlife values were naively used as a fulcrum whereby one culture tried to foist its priorities on another:

> The persuasion campaign was based on the American hypothesis that appreciation of wildlife is dependent on the awareness and knowledge of the subject. Africans did not accept conservation because educational materials were not similar to traditional persuasional devices. . . . Exposure to wildlife as aesthetically valuable was not sufficient to change the attitude that wildlife was basically a source of food.[5]

In terms of social equity, it is important to be clear about these differences of perception. They are not particularly racial, although many conservationists in Kenya are white. Rather, African rural values conflict with European conservationist predilections, which are alien and contrary to the prevailing interests expressed by most African agriculturists. The flavor of this non-African ethic is conveyed in the title to naturalist Bernhard Grzimek's now famous defense of the Tanzanian Serengeti, *Serengeti darf nicht sterben*, which can be alternatively translated as "Serengeti shall not die," "Serengeti must not die," and "Serengeti will not be permitted to die."[6] In Kenya as in Tanzania, no synthesis has been achieved between conservationist and grass-roots African sentiments, one reason being the lack of sympathy by conservationists for the human

3.2 Wildlife education bus in Nairobi National Park, 1970. World Wildlife Fund.

factor in the relationship. Most wildlife officers and many wildlife advocates are trained in biology, zoology, or some other natural science. Few take an interest in or have much understanding of the economic and political implications of the wildlife policies they favor. The sociology of wildlife in the human ecology of Kenya has yet to engage their attention at any but the most general level.

The culture conflict inherent in wildlife management is further exacerbated by racial imbalances in the wildlife "establishment." While only a few whites remain in official government positions, the broader conservation movement is heavily influenced by whites, both Kenyan citizens and expatriates. Attracted by a more favorable working environment than is found in Tanzania, many are professionals employed as researchers and veterinarians, or are foundation and United Nations personnel.

Most are "liberal" and sympathetic to African problems. At the same time, they are usually uneducated about local African cultures and economic systems, intimidated by senior African politicians, and reluctant to speak out on land-tenure and land-use problems because of their tenuous positions as outsiders. Although they may be concerned with human ecological issues, they avoid debate and thus exercise little influence over rural development policy.

Behind this group of more-or-less professional conservationists is a larger number of mainly white wildlife enthusiasts who have also flocked to Kenya. These are the amateur naturalists, publicists, and participants in the tourist industry who promote the glamorous aspects of wildlife as portrayed by extravagant safaris, white hunters, animal films, and coffee table photography books—a world that attracts and spends a great deal of money but which includes Africans mainly as drivers, bartenders, and game scouts. Again, such people may not be unsympathetic to African interests; they are simply ignorant of and dissociated from African problems as they appear on the ground. Common ground is rarely established between African peasants and the middle- and upper-class members of this informal wildlife establishment. One's definition of equity is the other's recipe for distress in the environmentally fragile and economically marginal ecosystems of Kenya's major wildlife areas.

A final, less savory group consists of the illicit exploiters of game animals, the poachers, and the other law breakers whose avarice and daring confound the legitimate wildlife establishment without benefiting those who must compete with wild animals for living space. The illegal wildlife establishment has become an ominous force that thwarts both governmental agencies and private groups seeking to perpetuate Kenya's game populations for either esthetic or scientific purposes, or as a means to earn revenues for improved agricultural land use.

Those groups that focus on both protecting wildlife and providing for impoverished and expanding rural populations offer the best chance of preserving wildlife. And yet, agricultural development seems as problematic at the periphery of human settlement as does effective game law enforcement. One important reason for this situation is that rural land users are far less organized and powerful than any segment of the Kenyan wildlife establishment.

The Wildlife Establishment and Kenyan Land Use

Kenya's geographical land-use distribution is summarized in Table 3.2. Less than 20 percent of the country is favored with sufficient soil fertility and rainfall to be considered naturally arable. These regions are densely populated, to the extent of endangering their natural endowments and of forcing a growing number of people into the semi-arid and arid locations making up the Kenyan agricultural periphery. Comprising most of the total land area, these reaches of scrubland, bush, and savanna surround the national parks and game reserves and the wildlife populations that increasingly compete with new settlements in the boundary zones that once separated humans and their livestock from protected game animals.

Technical innovation, economic assistance, and agricultural extension could help lessen this competition by enabling smallholders to intensify their cultivation and ranching activities at a safe distance from the parks and reserves. But this help has not been emphasized by the government which has lowered its relative commitment to agriculture in recent years and has concentrated its investments among "progressive" and often large-scale farms producing food and export crops in the fertile highlands. Across the entire sector, quantum inputs of fertilizers, feeds, seeds, and other resources fell by about 16 percent between 1978 and 1982. Be-

Table 3.2. Land Use in Modern Kenya

Land-Use Cateogry	Square Kilometers	Square Miles	Percent of Total Area
Naturally Arable	99,050	39,620	18
Agriculturally Peripheral, Settlement Permitted	425,621	170,248	75
National Parks and Game Reserves, Settlement Prohibited	39,491	15,797	7
Total Area[a]	564,162	225,665	100

[a]Excluding lakes.

tween 1978/1979 and 1981/1982, the amount of new agricultural credit
supplied to large farms declined from 4.6 million Kenyan pounds to 1.4
million pounds. The amount issued to the small farm majority was also
reduced, from 2.7 to 2.3 million pounds. Not surprisingly, the small farm
percentage of sales to official marketing boards decreased from 54.8 to
51.7 during the same period.[7]

Only 16 percent of the total agricultural population belonged to cooperative societies in 1980, and 75 percent of this minority was committed to nonfood export crops. Mainly because of changing urban tastes,
wheat flour consumption grew from 185,000 tons in 1978 to 243,000 tons
by 1982. Official wheat imports also increased, from 100,000 to 154,000
tons. In response, domestic wheat production was raised by 42 percent
during this time, from 157,000 tons to 223,000 tons.[8] Such trends favor
the large highland farms that are encouraged to specialize in commodities
for the urban and export markets. There is consequently even less attention paid to the agricultural periphery and to its problems of food, population, and environmental management.

Set against these realities is an officially recognized wildlife establishment that, at the periphery of human settlement, exerts a dispropor-
tionate influence as compared with similar interests in Tanzania and
other African countries containing large wildlife populations. An array
of governmental and nongovernmental, philanthropic and profit-making
organizations forms this lobby, and many of them use Kenya as a base
for operations throughout eastern Africa. These groups and their levels
of organization are indicated in Figure 3.2.

THE LEGAL WILDLIFE ESTABLISHMENT

International organizations working in the wildlife arena include several
United Nations and bilateral agencies, in addition to foundations and
other philanthropic groups. Most of their support is allocated to conservation projects, wildlife research, parks development, and equipment for
antipoaching units and wildlife training programs.

The most significant international conservation project of recent
years was funded by a $34 million World Bank loan for wildlife manage-
ment in the context of rural land use and development. As often happens
with large projects, the initial negotiations between donor and recipient

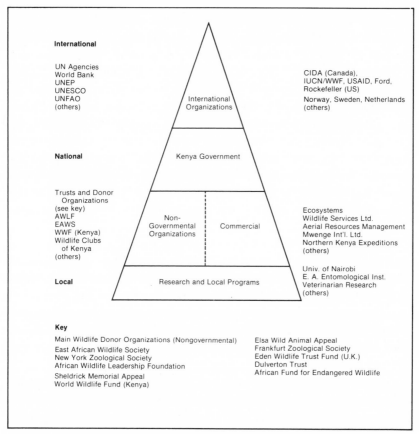

Key

Main Wildlife Donor Organizations (Nongovernmental)
East African Wildlife Society
New York Zoological Society
African Wildlife Leadership Foundation
Sheldrick Memorial Appeal
World Wildlife Fund (Kenya)

Elsa Wild Animal Appeal
Frankfurt Zoological Society
Eden Wildlife Trust Fund (U.K.)
Dulverton Trust
African Fund for Endangered Wildlife

Fig. 3.2. Kenya Wildlife Donor Organizations

agencies were protracted, and by the mid-1980s project activities are still minimal.[9] Certain indirect effects have been quickly felt, however. First, a wildlife planning unit was established for the first time, funded by supplementary Canadian aid. Second, the World Bank loan probably influenced the government's ban on hunting in 1977 and on the curio trade in wild animal products. Third, greater emphasis has been placed on the importance of land-use planning and human/livestock requirements near the parks and reserves. Finally, the government was persuaded to initiate a more efficient system of compensation for Maasai pastoralists who were moved from grazing areas close to Amboseli National Park and Maasai Mara National Reserve.

The Nairobi-based UN Environment Programme (UNEP) has also financed wildlife projects, in collaboration with UNESCO. UNEP helped produce a World Conservation Strategy in 1980 and, with UNESCO, sponsored Kenya's Integrated Project for Arid Lands, focusing on dry-lands ecology and carrying major implications for wildlife. The UN Centre for Human Settlement (Habitat) is likewise headquartered in Nairobi and has developed some interest in communities located in the peripheral areas also inhabited by wildlife. Another collaborator in the World Conservation Strategy, the International Union for Conservation of Nature and Natural Resources (IUCN), maintains an office in Nairobi and administers many of its eastern African projects from this base of operations. International foundations with a presence in Kenya, such as the Ford and Rockefeller foundations, occasionally sponsor wildlife projects as part of their philanthropic and developmental activities.

Kenyan government wildlife programs are mainly carried out by the Wildlife Conservation and Management Department of the Ministry of Environment and Natural Resources. Organizationally depicted in Figure 3.3, the department is charged with maintaining Kenya's thirty-seven national parks and game reserves, with managing eighteen other refuges for unique flora and fauna, and with providing public education, research and extension services, and policy planning. As Figure 3.4 suggests, the geographical scope of the department's jurisdiction is broad and varied. Tsavo National Park encloses 20,100 square kilometers (8,034 square miles), making it larger than the State of Israel. At the other extreme is the Saiwa National Park, with an area of only 192 hectares (480 acres).

Not unlike the situation in Tanzania, the wildlife's department's key performance difficulties involve routine management, infrastructural support, and staff morale. Salaries are low, promotions are slow in coming, cohesion is lacking, and cynicism runs high. One well-trained wildlife specialist, a helicopter pilot engaged in antipoaching work, resigned in 1981 not only because his salary was but a fraction of what Kenyan pilots usually earn, but also because he experienced constant problems of obtaining fuel, spare parts, and maintenance for his aircraft. He cited these terms of service as intolerable, even for a dedicated conservationist. Nevertheless, the Kenyan public wildlife sector is better organized and supported than its Tanzanian counterpart, and, like the international organizations located in Nairobi, makes its presence on behalf of wildlife protection felt in official policy-making circles.

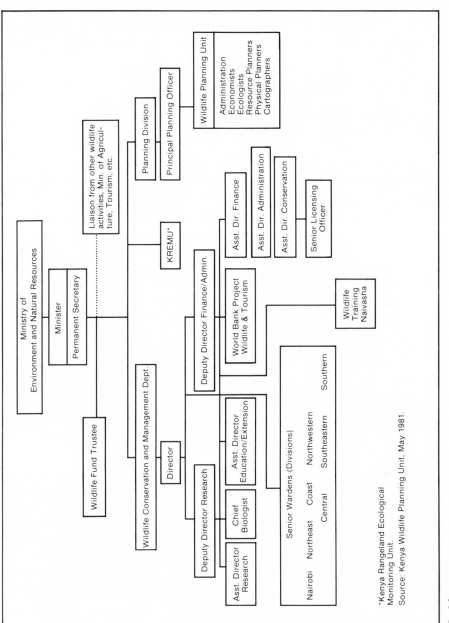

*Kenya Rangeland Ecological Monitoring Unit.

Source: Kenya Wildlife Planning Unit, May 1981.

Fig. 3.3.

Park and Reserve Names in Figure 3.4

1. Sibiloi National Park	18. Tsavo National Park
2. Marsabit National Reserve	19. South Kitui National Reserve
3. Losai National Reserve	20. Ngai Ndethya National
4. Samburu National Reserve	Reserve
5. Shaba National Reserve	21. Amboseli National Park
6. Meru National Park	22. Maasai Mara National
7. Bisanadi National Reserve	Reserve
8. Rahole National Reserve	23. Nairobi National Park
9. Kora National Reserve	24. Lambwe Valley National
10. North Kitui National	Reserve
Reserve	25. Ol Donyo Sabuk National
11. Arawale National Reserve	Park
12. Boni National Reserve	26. Mwea National Reserve
13. Dodori National Reserve	27. Mt. Kenya National Park
14. Kiunga Marine Reserve	28. Aberdare National Park
15. Tana River Primate	29. Lake Bogoria National Park
Reserve	30. Saiwa Swamp National Park
16. Malindi/Watamu Marine	31. Mt. Elgon National Park
Park	32. Nasalot National Reserve
17. Shimba Hills National	33. South Turkana National
Reserve	Reserve

NOTE: In addition to four other parks and reserves, 18 local sanctuaries for endangered flora and fauna, and seven forest reserves.

Nongovernmental organizations (NGOs) for the most part operate autonomously in Kenya, although they frequently cooperate with government wildlife officers on specific projects. These NGOs are engaged in a wide range of activities involving wildlife research and education; they provide scholarships, leadership training, equipment and vehicles for use in the parks, and funding in support of private efforts to preserve game and other wild animals.

As part of its larger work in Africa, the African Wildlife Foundation (AWF) serves as an administrative clearing house for private funds coming into Kenya from abroad. It supports projects to select and train wildlife professionals, mainly through scholarships and study tours, and handles equipment acquisitions for the parks and reserves. AWF also helps manage research projects and produces its own educational materials, including a widely read newsletter.

The East African Wildlife Society, founded in 1961, publishes a ma-

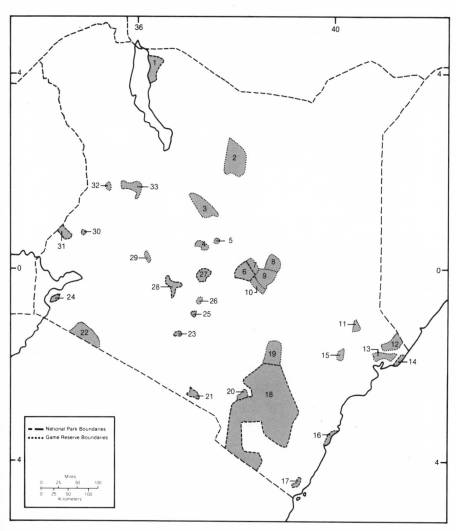

Fig. 3.4. Kenyan National Parks and Major Game Reserves

3.3   Wildlife research: the release of a young leopard wearing a radio monitoring collar, Kora National Reserve. David

jor journal, *Swara.* The society has supported research, supplied vehicles and other equipment to combat poaching, and served as a lobby for wildlife causes, especially in defense of the seriously endangered black and white rhinocerous.

The Wildlife Clubs of Kenya is an educational, youth-oriented organization with chapters throughout the country. Its primary function is to introduce wildlife topics into school curricula, and it supplements this undertaking with organized game park visits, lectures, and other activities.

A number of nongovernmental funds have also been established in Kenya, some broadly based and others to assist specific research in selected locations of the country. The New York Zoological Society, for example, finances the work of ecologist David Western; the Sheldrick Memorial Appeal was formed to commemorate the contributions of David Sheldrick, late park warden of Tsavo East. This fund focuses its spending on the Tsavo National Park.

Several wildlife consultative firms operate at the national level, most of them commercial operations that contract for research in technical fields such as aerial surveying or that engage in other specialized activities such as game cropping and animal enumeration. Many of these firms are headed by individuals who are either citizens or long-term residents of Kenya. Ian Parker's Wildlife Services Ltd., for instance, is basically a one-man enterprise that expands its staff when the need arises. Michael Rainy's Northern Kenya Expeditions Ltd., run by an American specialist on the Samburu area of northern Kenya, organizes safaris that offer a full range of educational services including field trips and ecological lectures. Some of these consultative operations maintain relations with larger overseas firms, and some use Kenya as a base for arranging contracts in other parts of eastern Africa.

Local research, much of it performed by expatriates, consists principally of short-term programs and special purpose projects funded by international and Kenyan sources. These activities vary from single-purpose studies by candidates for advanced degrees to more extensive research by teams investigating a particular species or ecosystem. Some of this work is quite protracted, such as the multiyear primatology project in Amboseli near Mt. Kilimanjaro. Dozens of wildlife researchers are scattered around Kenya at any given time.

As in other sectors of the wildlife establishment, little attempt has been made to integrate research efforts and to enhance their relevancy to human populations. A survey of 210 wildlife research projects initiated between 1968 and 1981 revealed several interesting findings, among them that of the first 137 projects carried out before 1972 only one dealt with human ecological concerns. Overall, only 4 of the 210 were so oriented.[10] Of all investigators listed, moreover, only seven were African. Most research was clustered into seven main categories; herbivores, predators, bird ecology, animal land use and range ecosystems, wildlife management and planning, aerial survey and range monitoring, and wildlife disease and veterinary studies.

While the stated purpose of many projects is to help wildlife managers make rational policy choices for specific species and ecosystems, a problem consistently reported during the compilation of this survey was the disjointed quality of the data. The great bulk of research frustrates planners and managers because of its scientific compartmentalization and its site-specific applicability. Only a few studies ever touch on the broader social, political, and economic issues that lie at the heart of Kenya's wildlife problems.[11]

The discussion to this point has been focused on that part of the wildlife establishment formally concerned with wild animals from a perspective combining philanthropy, education, science, and technology. Reconnoitering the informal side of the establishment plunges one into a sometimes bizzare world of profit making, local intrigue, and vested interests. Strong sentiments prevail, vestiges of the colonial past persist, and a racial structure survives through which a surprisingly large number of Europeans outside of government influences wildlife policy. Wildlife work remains a glamorous occupation in the tradition of bush suits, hunting safaris, and the ivory trade.

In Kenya, this group is made up of general conservationists, some government officers including game wardens and ex-wardens, a few foundation representatives, and a large contingent of writers, photographers, and other publicists. The informal establishment also includes an illegal assemblage of poachers, smugglers, illicit traders, and their white-collar manipulators. In terms of occupations, Figure 3.5 draws a rough distinction between scientific and nonscientific activities, with most of the informal establishment grouped into the "nonscience" quadrant. Wildlife occupations can also be classified according to their legality. The resulting four sectors are somewhat arbitrary in that they sometimes

3.4 Tourists viewing animals in middle-class comfort. UNEP.

overlap. The categorization is useful though as an approximation of the entire wildlife establishment.

Some of these occupations require further explanation. Rehabilitationists attempt to raise orphaned or wounded animals for eventual reintroduction into the wild. The late Joy Adamson's "born free" enterprises pertain here, as do George Adamson's present efforts to rehabilitate lions near Kora in northeastern Kenya and the Leslie-Melvilles' work with Rothchild giraffes. Preservationists share the interests of their Tanzanian counterparts and contend that natural habitats and animal species should be left totally undisturbed by humans. Conservationists advocate some preservationist views on specific species, but would allow human interaction with and exploitation of the wilderness while managing and protecting wild vegetation and animals.

Publicists form a category largely absent in Tanzania. Because wildlife have become such an important part of Kenya's capitalist economy, official tolerance has been granted to an enormous outpouring of picture books, popular accounts, and novels about primeval Africa. All this publicity represents big business, although scientists and informed citizens often lament its products as inaccurate, silly, and patronizing.

The final segment of the wildlife establishment may be insulting, but it is neither inaccurate in its knowledge about wildlife nor silly in the consequences of its actions. This group shares the others' dedication to wild animals, but in this instance dedication is expressed in terms of illegal exploitation for power and profit.

THE ILLEGAL WILDLIFE ESTABLISHMENT

Broadly viewed, several issues will continue to grip the Kenyan public policy system in the late 1980s and 1990s. These concerns include public and private sector elitism, widespread corruption and illegal economic activities, and simple law enforcement. Such problems are related and combine in many specific ways. At the juncture of wildlife protection and economic gain, they carry the potential for unprecedented damage to the country's most endangered ecosystems and to indigenous inhabitants.

Until his death in 1978, President Jomo Kenyatta presided over a government that functioned as an elite patronage system. The regime's constant need for additional patronage resources helps explain the warm official recognition extended to international commercial interests and to nonprofit wildlife organizations, the latter complementing an expanding tourist industry. Ironically, this same patronage requirement encouraged yet another set of indulgences that posed significant threats to Kenya's game animals and to some wildlife habitats. During the middle 1970s, the country was rocked by a series of revelations published in the *Sunday Times* of London. Three investigative reports exposed, among other improprieties, an extensive amassing of land holdings by the Kenyatta family and its close associates. Also uncovered was a pattern of senior bureaucratic profiteering at the expense of wildlife and the Kenyan ecosystem, involving large-scale ivory poaching and the destruction of forests to produce charcoal for sale in the Persian Gulf region.[12]

Wildlife-related corruption came to light at lesser levels as well and included widespread local poaching and smuggling, illegal auctions of wildlife products, and false official certification of such products for export. The extent of these offenses revealed a central tendency in Kenyan government and politics. A patronage system is particularly sensitive to shortages of rewards used to purchase the support of provincial and national leaders, local notables, and the masses of urban and rural dwellers. Drought, high fuel prices, and depressed international markets during the early 1970s severely depleted the domestic patronage larder, leading to a rapid growth in corrupt practices that engulfed whatever sources of profit remained. Game animals became one of these reservoirs, the exploitation of which seriously compromised the Kenyan policy emphasis on wildlife protection.

Today game officials, conservationists, and research ecologists agree that the poaching and trophy traffic has declined since its peak from 1970 to 1976. High officials implicated in the lucrative ivory, trophy, and skins trade gradually bowed to strong domestic and international pressure applied by the legal wildlife establishment. By the time President Daniel arap Moi assumed control in late 1978, wholesale export of these items had ceased. Since 1978 a number of additional factors has contributed to the further deterioration of this trade. President Moi's anticorruption campaign turned a spotlight on illicit governmental activities and has made large-scale profiteering more difficult. Ivory poachers, particularly Somalis hunting in Kenya, are experiencing greater difficulty getting elephant tusks out of the country. The antipoaching program, which has included deadly shootouts with sophisticated weapons, has negatively affected the poachers' cost-benefit calculations. The official closing of curio shops, far more than the hunting ban, has also made a difference. The prohibition on hunting has really curtailed only licensed shooting.

In spite of these gains, Moi officials point out that corruption, poaching, and smuggling persist in the wildlife areas. Part of the difficulty is that Kenya is not an isolated country; rather, it lies at the center of a thriving regional and international trade in wild animal products. Much illegal booty is still collected for markets in Europe, the Middle East, and Asia. Unquestionably, this traffic constitutes a major factor in the decline of some wildlife species.

The international trade in rhino products and ivory is especially significant in this regard. Although some seventy countries have signed a treaty to restrain trade in endangered species, much of the conservation message is lost on the purchasers of African animal products. In Asia, for example, the common attitude in the apothecary industry is that Africa

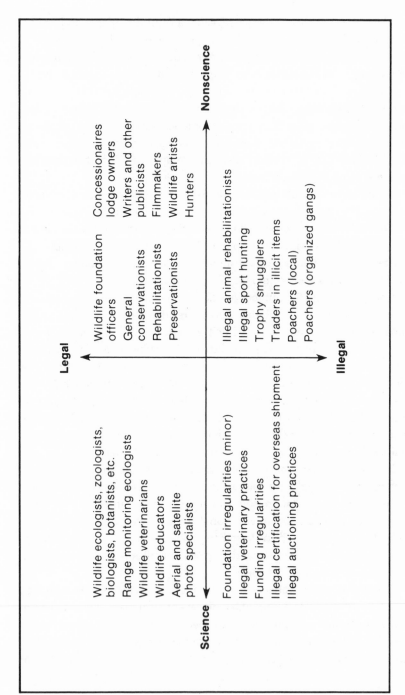

Fig. 3.5.

3.5 A suspected poacher's hideout. Kenya Information Service.

3.6 A poacher's trap and snare. World Wildlife Fund.

serves as an undeveloped and rather primitive source of useful primary commodities. Traffic in animal products is therefore justified as long as proper documentation is obtained. Interviewed in Nairobi, one Japanese trader put the point succinctly: "If Africans want to shoot their animals, that's their business. . . . We are businessmen and we will buy their products when they come on the legal market."

A large share of the trade in animal products is intended for medical and apothecary purposes. Japan, China, Malaysia, Indonesia, and India contain important markets for rhino horn, among other parts of these animals, used to make fever suppressants. Figure 3.6 profiles the oscillations of this trade with Japan. Hong Kong and Japan also import about 80 percent of all ivory sold on the world market, and in Japan five traders handle two-thirds of the national import. Japan has signed the endangered species treaty and buyers can import ivory only under license, but most customers neither know nor care if the export licenses are falsely certified. They view improper documentation as none of their business. Buyers will not act as policemen over themselves.

Although poachers, smugglers, and illicit traders receive most of the publicity and form the primary targets of law enforcement efforts, the illegal wildlife establishment also features white-collar crimes ranging from minor foundation funding irregularities to more serious licensing frauds. According to Ian Parker,

> the wildlife movement here is shot full of misguided people. Some of the "education and conservation" groups are so monocular that they have no idea of what they are preaching, to whom they are preaching, and what messages are actually being received. Some of the fund and donation organizations are so mismanaged that the pennies from our aunties in Chicago and Surrey never arrive. The donation game is, of course, not all a ripoff, but there are enough shrewd, semi-legal people in it to make it all questionable.[13]

To illustrate this problem, two case studies follow that are disguised versions of actual occurrences in the recent Kenyan experience. They suggest not only illegality, but also unfortunate slips in logic and the overpowering sentimentality often associated with wildlife advocacy.

Case I. The laws of Kenya prohibit catching and trapping game, except by special permit. Overseas sales are permitted only of animals born in

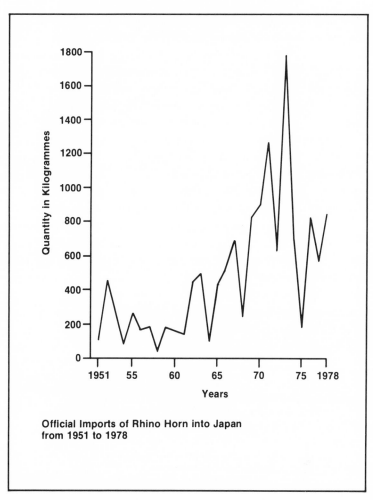

Fig. 3.6.

captivity. A wildlife entrepreneur receives a legitimate research grant to investigate the ethology of zebra, including grazing and mating behavior and the rearing of offspring. He also obtains official permission to herd a large number of zebra into observation pens for study. It turns out that only female zebra are brought into the pens, and most of these are pregnant. All zebra colts born in the pens are legally salable, and the entrepreneur realizes a windfall profit from marketing them to the world's zoos before the fraud is brought to light.

Case II. Large animal studies require sizeable grants, and one such award is made to a consulting group of seemingly well-established professionals. Without much review of the project or its investigators, a well-meaning foundation allocates a sum of money, deposited in the personal bank account of one of the consulting group's senior partners. The group subsequently dissolves in acrimony amid charges and countercharges of malfeasance. Legal moves to recover the grant are stymied by technicalities and by the foundation's embarrassed recalcitrance when some reports and analyses eventually appear.

Episodes of these kinds demonstrate the self-serving as well as altruistic motives inherent in Kenya's powerful wildlife establishment. Regardless of their intent, however, these interests tend to ignore and can even work at cross-purposes with the reforms that will determine whether wildlife ultimately survive in a natural state. In their single-minded exploitation of and lobbying for the animals, the several branches of the Kenyan wildlife establishment encourage a continued official neglect of the remaining factors in the country's man-land-wildlife equation—rural land users and the ecosystems they are destroying.

THE EMERGING LAND-USE CRISIS.

For some of those not forced to compete with them, Kenya's wild animals provide a basic psychological support. In the words of one such person,

> wildlife confirms our own lives and denies the destructive changes we perceive all around us. We fear society's rapid changes. We need benchmarks, reassurances that our own deaths are not immanent. Animals provide something of this. They are relics of the past that are still alive; and if they are bulldozed into oblivion, then our own existence is also threatened. When we get closer to the end of our string, we need reassurance about our own lives from wildlife. There is a symbolic reassurance in other living things, like a familiar landmark that convinces us we are still solid.[14]

Agriculturists living in or near the wildlife areas are permitted no such luxury. They are usually poor, smallholding peasants who fear and disdain wildlife not only because they destroy crops and livestock, but also because each year they kill and injure people, mainly women and children. Every time a woman treks to a river for water or to a distant

3.7   A menace to farmers: leopard at night. David Keith Jones.

field to work, she runs the risk of encountering a dangerous animal, a situation that can keep a community in a state of constant agitation.

Even when not threatened with overpopulation and environmental depletion, rural communities often exhibited belief systems whose negative images were animal forms. These traditional beliefs still include a powerful myth-based denigration of animals, who are associated with supernatural powers, witchcraft, and illness. Clay figures and wood carvings of hideous beasts are yet employed as teaching devices in some local cultures. Jackals, hyenas, crocodiles, and other dreaded creatures are portrayed as witches in disguise or as controlled by witches, who are also believed to be able to transform people into these forms.

Animal-based fears, like fears of illness and natural disaster, are part of the traditional uncertainty confronting people in the agriculturally poor areas of Kenya. Today, population growth and rural overcrowding produce additional anxieties. These changes occur faster than rural dwellers can absorb with their own resources, and wildlife are caught up in the process. When peasants are required to alter their agricultural practices without externally provided assistance, they must likewise revise their attitudes toward themselves and their habitats. Less accommodating and ecologically symbiotic than before, they are compelled to brutalize their environmental commons through overcropping, overgrazing, and an indiscriminate killing of wild animals they now perceive as competitors for the same space.

Statistical averages offer some measure of these circumstances. Table 3.3 presents estimates of population growth and density in those parts of Kenya that contain the most fertile soils and typically receive the greatest amount of annual rainfall. Several conclusions can be drawn from these data. First, protected game animals and human populations generally favor the same territory, which represents 80 percent of the nearly 100,000 square kilometers (40,000 square miles) naturally arable. This statistic shows the association of wildlife with people to be closer than in Tanzania with that country's more dispersed pattern of arable land. In 1985, more than 60 percent of the Kenyan population was estimated to be living in administrative provinces that include the majority of national parks and reserves. In these and other provinces, moreover, population and density virtually doubled in the fifteen years between 1969 and 1985, and are expected to double again in the fifteen years from 1985 to 2001.

Table 3.3. Kenyan Population Growth and Density in Relation to Arable Land

Province	Population, (000) 1969	1985[a]	Arable Land (km²)/ Percent of Total	Density (per km²) Total 1969	1985[a]	Arable 1969	1985[a]
			Major Wildlife Provinces				
Central	1,676	3,042	9,240/2	127	231	181	330
Coast	944	1,749	11,480/2	11	22	61[b]	152[b]
Eastern	1,907	3,534	26,920/5	12	23	71	131
Rift Valley	2,210	4,095	31,480/6	32	58	70	130
Total	6,737	12,420	79,120/15 *Average*	46	84	96	186
			Other Provinces				
Nairobi	509	998	–	745	1,459	–	–
North-Eastern	246	456	–	2	4	–	–
Nyanza	2,122	3,932	12,520/2	169	314	169	314
Western	1,328	2,461	7,410/1 *Average*	162	299	179	332
Total	4,205	7,847	19,930/3	270	519	174	323

[a]Rounded estimates.
[b]Excluding Mombasa Municipality totaling 210 square kilometers.

SOURCES: Kenya, *Kenya Fertility Survey, 1977–1978*, Volume 1 (Nairobi: Central Bureau of Statistics, Ministry of Economic Planning and Development, 1980). p. 5; and World Bank, *Toward Sustained Development in Sub-Saharan Africa* (Washington: The World Bank, 1984), pp. 82, 85.

Nonwildlife provinces fall into three broad categories: heavily urbanized (Nairobi), so dry as to be unarable under natural conditions
(North-Eastern), and highly arable but also very densely settled (Nyanza
and Western). Because of their land pressures, Nyanza and Western
provinces are contributing a steady flow of rural migrants to the east, especially into Rift Valley and Central provinces with their large numbers
of game sanctuaries and their own human density problems in the vicinities of some of these refuges. Average densities vary in the wildlife provinces and reflect different aggregate carrying capacities. Here, average
annual rainfall ranges from less than 250 millimeters (10 inches) to about
1270 millimeters (51 inches), as compared with a range of from about 760
millimeters (30 inches) to more than 1780 millimeters (71 inches) in
Nyanza and Western provinces.[15] With the exceptions of northern Rift
Valley and northwestern Coast, where no parks or reserves are located,
these provinces have already exceeded, have reached, or are quickly
reaching their limits of agricultural carrying capacity with the productive
technologies currently available.[16]

Demographic statistics tell part but not all of the story. To gain a
fuller appreciation of Kenya's impending land-use crisis and its implications for wildlife areas, and to understand what these areas mean to the
country, it is necessary—as in Tanzania—to move closer and examine the
problems of land use at this grass-roots level.

Wildlife and Land Use at Ground Level

It is difficult to overestimate the importance of land in rural Kenya. As I
have earlier argued,

> a land fever grips Kenyans and intertwines both modern and
> traditional values. No other issue is so political or so explosive.
> Who has land, who gets land, who buys and sells land—and
> when and for what price—are the perennial sources of discussion
> at all levels of the society. The deep-seated consciousness about
> land is based on land shortage, landlessness, and the social
> inequities bred by land problems. Land offers basic survival
> opportunities in an insecure world. Land is welfare when there is
> no welfare system. Land is wealth when no other forms of wealth
> are available.[17]

Against these local interests wildlife may stand little chance, in spite of Kenya's powerful wildlife lobby in Nairobi. Yet the very land so vital to everyone's needs is rapidly becoming useless to all.

As Capone has pointed out, man's greatest negative impact on wildlife species results not from poaching and other illegal utilization, but rather from environmental changes brought about by intensive farming and pastoralism without the benefits of modern technologies.[18] Each activity disrupts natural vegetation, which in turn destroys indigenous food balances and can lead to quick declines in some wild animal populations, to sudden increases in others, and to extinction for still others. Cultivation replaces the natural cover with a few domesticated crops, and herding gives rise to selective shortages of certain grassland plants. Applied too intensively, both practices reduce soil fertility and promote erosion and, in arid locations, desertification. Firewood gathering and charcoal making deplete woody habitats and encourage soil run-off, as do field clearing and bush burning designed to help generate new grass for livestock.

These disturbances were minimized when rural populations remained widely scattered across the frontier areas claimed by game animals. Today such changes become crises for the animals and for the land-hungry peasants who created them in the first place. Even in the absence of densely settled villages of the sort artificially created in Tanzania, carrying capacities have been drastically lowered for animals and rural dwellers as the latter push steadily toward the parks and reserves. Deprived of their migratory expansion areas, compressed populations of game animals wreak havoc on these protected ecosystems.

This tragedy of the commons has been developing for some time in many Kenyan localities, as in similar parts of Tanzania. Capone reported on several crisis situations as they appeared during the late 1960s, in provinces containing nearly 80 percent of the country's major parks and reserves. Amboseli National Park is located in Kajiado District of Rift Valley Province, which encloses five other national parks and reserves. In 1979, Kajiado displayed an average population density of only seven people per square kilometer, in an area of 19,605 square kilometers (7, 842 square miles). Although this density was even lower in the 1960s, Capone was still able to observe considerable environmental damage caused by excessive livestock populations. Before Amboseli was converted into a full-fledged national park, large portions of its territory were available to Maasai pastoralists for grazing. As an example of wild-life conservation problems in pastoral areas, Capone noted that

> the [Amboseli Game] Reserve is badly overstocked and has suffered from severe overgrazing and erosion. The Maasai are tolerant of wildlife and their cattle have always shared the range peacefully with wild grazing animals. The wild grazers consume different food plants from those eaten by cattle and so do not compete directly with the Maasai stock. But the heavy grazing pressure of the large numbers of cattle has lowered the carrying capacity of the range and resulted in a marked reduction of wildlife populations.[19]

Livestock are no longer permitted to range peacefully in Amboseli, but the ravages of overgrazing continue at the park's outskirts. Within, growing populations of wild ungulates take up where the livestock left off.

Wildlife in marginal farming areas face like threats. Sedentary culti-vation works to reduce large-animal populations, in some cases to the point of extinction, and most game animals are large. Where agricultur-alists are densely settled near the parks and reserves, land use is particu-larly intense, and so is the competition between cultivators and game animals. Under these circumstances, park and reserve boundaries afford little protection to endangered wildlife, and local pressures mount for of-ficial interventions to control (i.e., shoot) "excessive numbers" of species such as hippopotamus, rhinocerous, buffalo, lion, and leopard. Fencing off wildlife is a very expensive and therefore impractical solution to the problem, although it has been practiced in a few places such as portions of the Aberdare National Park. By confining the animals within tightly circumscribed enclosures, moreover, they themselves may be compelled to overexploit their habitats. But such difficulties are only rarely encoun-tered. Most examples of wildlife-peasant conflict develop according to scenarios portrayed in the Shimba Hills, Lambwe Valley, and northern Tsavo experiences.

The Shimba Hills National Reserve is situated in the Kilifi and Kwale districts of southeastern Coast Province, which contains eight ad-ditional parks and reserves. Totaling 20,671 square kilometers (8,268 square miles) of semi-arable wooded grassland and coastal forest, Kilifi and Kwale are the scenes of long-standing human population pressures. In 1952, the colonial administration responded to these pressures by es-

3.8 Wildlife control officers in training, Tsavo National Park. World Wildlife Fund.

tablishing a resettlement scheme in the Shimba Hills below a forest reserve protecting a variety of game species (including the rare sable
antelope).

Writing nearly two decades later, Capone described what has e-
merged as a familiar situation where land-hungry peasants confront
wildlife.

> Demand for game control by the settlers has been high and
> buffalo and elephant, especially, are shot in substantial numbers.
> Poaching is also a problem and it has been reported that the
> villagers below the reserve deliberately burn the grass on the
> lower slopes to attract sable, buffalo, and other grazing animals.
> The Shimba Hills Reserve is a relatively small area and the game
> populations it supports are not large. The sable antelope in
> particular number less than 100 animals in the reserve and this
> small group is the largest concentration of sable left in Kenya.[20]

Shimba Hills is now administered as a national park to help save the
sable antelope and other species, but human population densities in Kilifi
and Kwale rose from the lower thirties per square kilometer during the
late 1970s to the middle forties by the mid-1980s. The future of Shimba
Hills National Reserve is now cast into serious doubt, as are the future
prospects for subsistence farming in Kilifi and Kwale districts.

The Lambwe Valley Game Reserve was gazetted during the 1960s to
enhance the life chances of various southwestern species of wildlife, in
particular, another rare antelope—the roan. This reserve remains
Nyanza Province's only game sanctuary and is one of the smallest in
Kenya. Occupying a six by forty-kilometer (four by twenty-five-mile)
strip of land in South Nyanza District, Lambwe Valley coexists with a
highly concentrated rural population whose average density exceeds 180
per square kilometer and 55 per square kilometer in Lambwe proper.

Lambwe Valley was once protected by the tsetse fly, but severe land
shortages forced settlers into the area and prompted the government to
designate it as a game reserve. Squatters moving into the reserve stimu-
lated the government's next step —declaring the valley a de facto national park. Just before this latter step was taken, Capone suggested that
"expulsion of the squatters and fencing the reserve will probably be necessary if the Lambwe Valley Game Reserve is to survive at all."[21] Today
Lambwe survives, but the continued existence of its wildlife inhabitants
is far from assured.

Machakos District encompasses a large territory of 14,178 square kilometers (5,671 square miles) in Eastern Province and also includes northern portions of the Tsavo National Park. At an average density of about ninety people per square kilometer, Machakos is heavily populated for the natural carrying capacity of its grassland, scrub, and thicket environment. Similar human-ecological limitations partly account for the fact that Eastern Province contains nine other national parks and reserves, for a total number exceeding that of any other province.

Like the Lambwe Valley, southern Machakos is affected by the tsetse fly, and this natural obstacle once protected the northern Tsavo from large human and livestock populations. Beginning in the early 1960s, an influx of new settlement was encouraged by the "push" of increasing populations and densities elsewhere in Machakos, and by improving rainfall and water supply conditions, an upgrading of the main Nairobi-Mombasa road, and an officially sanctioned resettlement scheme. By the middle to late 1960s, these factors had led to decreasing agricultural carrying capacities in the vicinity of the park, to serious disruptions of natural vegetation caused by charcoal production as a cottage industry, and to yet other ecological imbalances that profoundly altered the abundance and distribution of several large ungulate species, of elephant, and especially of rhinocerous. Human land pressures have grown relentlessly in more recent years. Between 1979 and 1985 alone, average densities in the Kikumbulyu hinterland area of Tsavo climbed from twenty-two to about thirty people per square kilometer.

From his detailed study of these forces at work in Kikumbulyu, Capone was led to conclusions that remain pregnant with general implications for the Kenyan public policy process. Unfortunately, these issues have yet to be addressed.

In Kenya, with its limited natural resource base, prudence would seem to dictate that the wisest use be made of the resources available. To replace wild animals with subsistence agriculture in marginal areas where agricultural experts agree that permanent agriculture cannot succeed is, in ecological terms, unwise land use policy. Economically, wildlife is certainly one of Kenya's most valuable resources, contributing substantially to the national income at the present time and capable of greatly increased contribution in the future. Considering the paucity of other resources available, it may not be overstating its value to view the conservation of wildlife as indispensible to the economic development of Kenya.[22]

3.9   Flamingos, cattle, and homesteads in southern Nyanza Province.   David Keith Jones.

The point is well taken but one may differ with Capone as to the complete irrationality of subsistence (and cash-crop) agriculture in the peripheral areas required by wildlife. Although such land-use practices may not be desirable in an ideal world, they are surely inevitable in modern Kenya. The real dilemma facing the Kenyan policy system is how to balance land-use needs and wildlife protection without denying either.

The Critical Policy Issues

Kenya's development strategy is biased toward capitalism and relies more heavily on private economic initiative than Tanzania's. In spite of this difference, the Kenyan and Tanzanian economies share two characteristics in common: their essentially statist patterns of investment and management and their consistent neglect of agriculture. Even though Kenya's economic affairs are subjected to fewer controls than Tanzania imposes, the state remains the main provider and coordinator of productive resources. As such, its influence over the agricultural sector is nearly as great as that exercised in Tanzania. Also in common with Tanzania, the budgetary position of agriculture is unusually low in relation to the contribution of agriculture to the national income. Table 3.4 shows that, between 1980/1981 and 1983/1984, an average of about 14.5 percent of the Kenyan national budget was allocated to agriculture (including forestry and fisheries), while 23 percent was committed to other economic activities (principally industry, utilities, communications, and physical infrastructure), 42 percent to social infrastructure (education, health, housing, and welfare), and 17 percent to defense.[23] Short-term spending trends suggest equally obvious distortions when agriculture is compared with defense and, to a lesser extent, general administration.

This situation starkly contrasts with a reality presently receiving much scrutiny from quarters that normally pay little heed to Africa and its development problems. In one recent statement, the Office of Technology Assessment of the United States Congress offered the following views on Africa's current food crisis:

> The greatest potential for significantly expanding...food production lies in increasing the productivity of small, subsistence-level farmers and herders, who raise most of Africa's food and yet have been largely ignored. Food producers need

Table 3.4. Kenyan National Budget Expenditures, 1980–1984
(percent of total spending)

Sector	1980/1981	1981/1982	1982/1983[a]	1983/1984[a]
Agriculture, Forestry, and Fishing	16.4	13.9	14.5	13.2
Mining, Manufacturing, and Construction	5.3	3.9	4.1	5.5
Electricity, Gas, Steam, and Water	6.2	6.0	4.1	5.2
Roads	8.7	10.4	9.0	8.1
Transport and Communications	1.4	1.7	1.6	2.0
Other Economic Services	2.6	2.5	2.0	1.8
Education	26.6	26.4	28.3	27.0
Health	9.8	9.5	9.6	9.1
Housing and Community Welfare	2.2	2.0	0.7	0.9
Social Welfare	3.3	3.4	4.4	4.4
Defense	13.5	17.5	19.0	17.2
General Administration	4.1	3.3	2.7	6.0

NOTE: Percentages may not total 100 because of rounding.
[a]Provisional.
SOURCE: Kenya, *Economic Survey 1984* (Nairobi: Central Bureau of Statistics, Ministry of Finance and Planning, 1984), p. 80.

technologies which are low risk, low input, such as commercial fertilizer, based on existing agricultural methods, and suitable for small farms, small businesses, and small incomes in Africa.... The challenge is to devise research, extension and aid programs that involve local people and integrate on-farm work into the larger framework of national and international affairs.[24]

As these conclusions were announced, Kenya was joined by Tanzania and twelve other African countries as needing historically unprecedented quantities of food aid to ward off the famine and mass starvation that had already overtaken Chad, Ethiopia, Mali, Mauritania, and Mozambique.[25]

Because such a large proportion of Kenya's area is infertile and such a large number of its food producers are subsistence peasants, low-level technologies and economic services applied as widely as possible are indispensable to the amelioration of the country's periodic food shortages and to the resolution of its longer-range nutritional and environmental difficulties. Both the latter problems are especially critical in the four provinces that enclose most of the major game parks and reserves. In the late 1970s, over 30 percent of all children in Central, Coast, Eastern, and Rift Valley provinces suffered from serious height-per-age deficiencies associated with chronic food deprivation.[26] Throughout the peripheral areas that also support wildlife, overcultivation and overgrazing have caused environmental disturbances that in some places may have already reached irreversible levels.

In Eastern Province, for example, large numbers of squatters follow their traditional pattern of shifting agriculture, but at settlement densities that compel them to cultivate the same plots for three or more years. Deprived of relevant extension advice, fertilizers, and irrigation, these peasants quickly exhaust the land and then move on to repeat the process. The results seem particularly apparent in Machakos and neighboring Kitui districts, where productive inputs are seldom employed, where water catchments have become depleted, where crop failures are common, and where soil erosion is widespread.[27] In the pastoral regions to the west, Kenya is already more densely populated with humans and livestock than are the pastoral areas of Tanzania and other countries in the eastern African cattle complex.[28] To an even greater extent than in Tanzania, restricted grazing opportunities force Kenyan herders to overstock their range and also to form group ranching schemes that further consolidate and confine their stock. These latter ventures are undertaken with official encouragement, but without much in the way of technical assistance and controls to insure optimal grazing quotas as determined by range capacity and water availability.

Human pressures and policy shortcomings appear largely responsible for the significant declines that have affected certain wildlife populations in recent years. Kenya's large herbivores presently number about three million, many fewer than in previous decades. A proliferation of sedentary farming communities has reduced the grazing territory of these animals and has interfered with their periodic migratory routes in the game controlled areas that serve as expansion zones beyond the parks and reserves. The constant addition of domestic livestock has produced the same effects and has led to increasingly direct competition for forage and water. Large predators, necessary to maintain delicate balances between wild ungulates and their food supplies, are driven from densely settled locations or simply exterminated.

Combined with the depredations of poachers and the lobbying efforts of Kenya's wildlife establishment, the growing preponderance of peasants over wildlife led to the official hunting ban of 1977. Licensed hunting originally offered some benefits to rural dwellers. Fees were collected on animals shot in game controlled areas, helping to support the administrative and developmental activities of local district councils and to reimburse farmers for animal damage to their crops. The fees are no longer paid, and by the mid-1980s large ungulate and predator populations have grown to the point of causing serious crop damage in some localities. Peasant demands have mounted to reinstate hunting in the game controlled areas, to which farmers and pastoralists hold title under customary, leasehold, and freehold land-tenure arrangements.[29]

The dynamics of agricultural land use and the threats posed to Kenya's wildlife raise several major policy issues. From a purely technical standpoint, agricultural output can be increased by two to four times its current yields. Such gains would accommodate Kenya's growing population and help satisfy its labor requirements for some time to come. Increased yields can be accomplished by expanding arable land and intensifying agricultural production, employing means that protect the rural environment and also allow room for wildlife. These innovations must begin with applied research into improved crop packages, cropping systems, and land management practices, backed by price incentives for food crops and by initial investments to develop low-potential areas not inhabited by game animals.[30]

Research should be extended to the wildlife areas as well. For example, investigations of the Maasai Mara National Reserve have determined that additional knowledge is required on many subjects of great ecological importance to both rural dwellers and animals. These subjects include the nature of lion behavior, the impact of grass and bush burning and of tourists and their infrastructure, the migratory patterns of selected bird species, the role of elephant in range destruction, various aspects of game physiology, pathology, and epidemiology, and external human influences over the reserve—particularly those exerted by nearby Maasai group ranching schemes.[31]

Before the technical issues can be resolved, certain social and political obstacles must be overcome. First, the confrontational attitude of government toward the relationship of people to wildlife must be replaced by one emphasizing the potential contributions of both peasants and game animals to Kenya's future prosperity. The government has acknowledged the need for this change, reversing a mindset dating back to a time when colonial wildlife officers met every human challenge to game animals with force. Today, "Wildlife Service Officers must cease to be mainly policemen, telling landowners what they cannot do, and increasingly become their advisers."[32] This recognition is not yet well represented in the implementation of wildlife policies.

In addition, some of the wildlife establishment's more eccentric and sometimes dangerous preoccupations should probably be curtailed. Perhaps the most controversial activities in this category involve the rehabilitation of wounded and orphaned game animals, raising them in close contact with humans and thereafter returning them to the wild. Nearly all professional wildlife specialists agree that such rescue operations, particularly to save big cats, are unnatural and hazardous undertakings and carry immediate risks for people living within eighty kilometers (fifty miles) of where the rehabilitations take place. John Seago, one of Kenya's highly respected conservationists who once made a living by capturing wild animals for zoos and for scientific research, has stressed the danger to all concerned when partially tamed and naturally unequipped animals are reintroduced to the bush.[33] This non-African penchant is highly insensitive and irresponsible to the security needs of nearby African communities and only reinforces the traditional view of game animals as enemies to be destroyed when avoiding them becomes impossible.

Other conflicts of interest between rural dwellers and wildlife advocates will likewise have to be resolved. As in Tanzania, these differences reflect as yet unanswered questions to which both groups provide ready but uninformed responses. The human presence always carries with it some ecological implications, and no one is quite sure how much "preservation" is necessary to sustain wildlife in their eastern African habitats. No one knows the specific survival capabilities of individual species, so each side of the wildlife/land-use debate prefers to err at the extremes. The wildlife establishment argues either for the complete insulation of wild animals from human interference or for conservation through strictly limited game cropping. Farmers and herders insist on a drastic reduction and even a total elimination of game populations. The fact remains that neither side is exactly sure when a species' reproductive capacity is threatened or when the carrying capacity of the land is exceeded by wildlife.

Closely associated with the question of game cropping is the current

discussion over whether to allow the controlled hunting of certain supposedly overabundant mammals and birds, with the understanding that
landowners would become direct beneficiaries by receiving payment
from hunters killing these animals on their land. Supporters argue that
cropping is critical in some areas and that controlled hunting would
present a new resource for rural development. Opponents point out that
controlled utilization promotes uncontrolled exploitation and that licensing irregularities and other imperfections appear when any hunting is allowed.

Excluding a few clear cases—roan and sable antelope and rhinocerous, for instance—a controversy also rages about which species are actually endangered. Does this term mean "not found in places where they
were formerly encountered"? If so, crocodile, flamingo, leopard, cheetah, and more than a dozen other species may be endangered. If the designation means "endangered unto extinction," then a different set of
animals may be involved. Sounding the alarm over species thought to be
endangered, then discovering they are breeding in greater numbers than
before, undermines the credibility of all wildlife concerns. The old adage
applies: if wildlife representatives cry wolf too often, soon no one will
listen.

The vastness of Kenya and the fact that thousands of square kilometers have been set aside for parks and reserves make effective game management difficult at best. Borders are constantly breached, poaching
continues unabated, and animals constantly encroach upon farming and
grazing land. Game moats, dikes, fences, and other barriers have not
proved to be very effective prevention devices. How to protect game
from outraged peasants remains a serious dilemma across Kenya. Most
game officials believe that firm economic priorities will have to be set for
animal populations and their territories adjusted accordingly. Most also
think that wildlife will ultimately have to be physically separated from
human communities. The ways, means, and possible consequences of
these actions have not yet been politically determined.

One example of the political difficulties encountered when confronting these problems would include Kenya's use of group ranches for the
pastoral Maasai. This complicated policy was established to gain accep-
tance for and to administer restricted grazing in designated locations

around the parks and reserves. The plan, at the same time, enables the Maasai to share in the revenue generated from park fees. To enhance its legitimacy, the scheme is administered by local Maasai county councils in Narok and Kajiado districts. This governing system means that the central government wildlife division is frequently plunged into the *realpolitik* of the Maasai councils. The land politics of "who gets what, when, where, and how" are played out as fiercely here as in any other part of Kenya. The government's interest lies in protecting the game and the tourist earnings such create, but this interest is the lesser of several goals motivating land-conscious Maasai politicians. The leadership a central government can exercise and that which must be left to local initiatives represents an equation requiring delicate balancing and rebalancing of competing group interests.

Perhaps the thorniest issue of all, and one that gives rise to these other quandaries, concerns the debate over what constitutes the best possible use of Kenya's land area. As Ian Parker and others have observed, population densities and the vagaries of rainfall undergird an inexorable process of migration, colonization, and exploitation. As long as man needs more land to feed his progeny, only the limits of physical possibility, largely defined by water and soil, will deter his expansion. Wildlife are expendable if the need is great enough and cannot be absorbed through an environmentally compatible intensification of agriculture.

Much of Kenya's recent history revolves around the twin issues of land hunger and population growth. The average rural couple desires and begets eight to ten children. Decisions on the number of children to have are still based on expectations of high infant and child mortality and on anticipated old-age security through family self-help. Although modern medicine has dramatically increased infant and child survival rates, and although the public sector is increasingly able to provide for the basic needs of rural dwellers, the country's lagging rural development has not yet reduced the uncertainties of subsistence and controlled fertility by creating economic alternatives to child bearing. The result is a compelling pressure to obtain whatever land can be pressed into service for the survival and security of large families.

As in Tanzania and throughout tropical Africa, overcoming rural poverty forms the most basic policy project of modern Kenya. Solutions to all other issues of land use and wildlife protection hinge upon this project's outcomes. Whether the Kenyan policy system is up to the challenge can legitimately be questioned.

Conclusion: Policy System Constraints

Regardless of the "purist" sentiments strongly expressed by the scientific and esthetic wings of Kenya's wildlife establishment, tourist revenues provide the raison d'etre for officially supported wildlife protection. Should this economic justification fail, enormous political pressures would mount to open the game parks and reserves to human settlement. A collapse of the tourist industry, however, could be provoked by any number of events, including rural economic failure, urban political upheaval, and, conceivably, mass hunger and starvation. All parts of the man-land-wildlife relationship are closely linked, and the problem is where to intervene. Under the circumstances of Kenya, as well as Tanzania, the answer lies in the countryside.

Kenya's most aggressive agrarian policy of the 1970s was the Special Rural Development Programme (SRDP). This project was intended to coordinate the work of all relevant ministries and local agencies on behalf of a nationwide attempt at integrated rural development. Although administrative personnel were dispersed to the rural areas, policy-making authority remained in Nairobi. Individual projects lacked adequate baseline data on local conditions, and peasant farmers were rarely consulted about project design and implementation. SRDP also became susceptible to the patronage requirements of Kenya's senior politicians, which further reduced its developmental impact as individual projects were allocated to reinforce constituency ties rather than to improve local living conditions, to reform agricultural land-use practices, and to increase crop and livestock production.

Representing the World Bank, Uma Lele evaluated the SRDP as it had evolved by the middle 1970s.

> The allocation of resources is increasingly being influenced by technical and national party considerations rather than by local needs or constraints. As the preceding experience of SRDP

indicates, the neglect of local input has had an unfavorable effect on the performance of the rural development effort....Proper procedures have to include consultation with rural residents, careful identification of local needs and constraints, intelligent application of appropriate technical and institutional criteria, and a feedback mechanism to assess progress and to remove obstacles in the way of its realization. The successful institution of such procedures is, however, frequently blocked by bureaucratic inertia and political pressures that result in following or abandoning programs irrespective of their intrinsic merit.[34]

Because policy elites and peasants went their separate ways, precious infrastructure and productive resources were wasted, and the land became less and less able to support its inhabitants. Ecological failures helped create economic reversals that, in turn, disrupted political stability throughout Kenya. As the land neared exhaustion in some areas, human and non-human land users experienced stresses that threatened them with famine.

Upon his assumption of power in 1978, President Moi sought to control if not eliminate Kenya's "informal" political and economic systems by distributing offices more representatively among the country's ethnic groups, by removing flagrantly corrupt officials, and by attempting to create an improved climate for foreign investment. During the early 1980s, his efforts were impeded by three closely related ecological factors—population growth and urbanization, terminal shortages of arable land, and drought. Soil erosion, deforestation, and desertification had invaded large parts of the densely populated west and the demographically expanding north. Land-tenure litigations and violent ethnic clashes over land rights had become commonplace in the western highlands. Food scarcity had grown to such an extent that, in its urban manifestation, it provided one justification for the attempted air force coup of August 1982.

In 1983, an increasingly desperate Moi administration raised the official producer price for maize by 30 percent, leading to a record planting made possible by the widespread opening of environmentally fragile new lands. Except in a few locations, the rains failed in 1983 and again in 1984. The critical central highlands received less than 30 percent of the rainfall necessary to produce a normal maize crop, and by late 1984 Western diplomats and aid officials estimated that at least 1.5 million tons of grain would have to be imported if massive hunger was to be avoided before the next harvest. This tonnage equalled three times the amount Kenya had imported in any previous year. It would cost about $250 million, a sum that about matched the treasury's total foreign-exchange reserves. The previous July, the minister for labor accused un-named senior officials of hoarding food to sell when the crisis grew worse. At the end of that month, the government embargoed further grain exports and launched a search of storage facilities for hoarded grain products. This action failed to prevent the disappearance of thirty-four truckloads of maize from a government depot in Nairobi.[35] As all these events were unfolding, tourist numbers to the national game parks declined by about 6 percent.[36]

In the face of these difficulties, the Kenyan government has announced its intention to achieve food self-sufficiency, to reduce the scope of political and bureaucratic control over the rural sector, to encourage local productivity through incentives such as consistently higher producer prices and improved agricultural services, and to promote environmentally sensitive self-help activities voluntarily led, wherever necessary, by private expatriates who can provide the locally unavailable skills.[37] These reforms are critical to the accommodation, in a finite commons, of inexorably growing human populations and threatened wildlife species. With the release of grass-roots energies from bureaucratic lethargy and political expedience, peasants could be persuaded to abandon their increasing aversion to formal economic participation (which in the present sense often means exploitation) and to enter a new age of entrepreneurship and ecological stewardship.

Will rural dwellers respond in this manner? This answer is uncertain because no one has yet consulted them. Until now, Kenyan peasants have suffered as much from a policy of benign neglect as have Tanzanian smallholders from a transformational strategy that has not worked. In both countries, the unfortunate truth remains that no synthesis has yet been reached of national wildlife priorities and local African needs. The experience of Kenya suggests that such a synthesis is central to the prevention of future disasters for human society, for wildlife, and for the public policy system that must finally be held accountable for the consequences of its decisions and nondecisions.

4
Land-Use and Wildlife
Policy in Perspective:
Competing Demands and
Uncertain Capacities

Overview: Linkage Problems in Wildlife and Land-Use Policy

In both Tanzania and Kenya, people and wild animals are subjected to life-threatening ecological stresses. These tensions are linked to a common physical environment and unfold in zero sum fashion. As one group gains a temporary advantage in its struggle to survive, the other suffers a setback. Evidence suggests that humans and other species respond similarly to such pressures, sometimes in unexpected ways. In his studies of alcoholism, psychiatrist Ronald Siegal has observed that elephants as well as humans consume intoxicants in direct proportion to their personal insecurities—caused for elephants by reductions in herding areas leading to overcrowding and food scarcity. Siegal concludes that "environmental stress can be an important variable in the self-administration of alcohol [from fermented fruits and grains] in these natural habitats. Elephants drink, perhaps, to forget...the anxiety produced by shrinking

115

rangeland and the competition for food. And I think that we can see a little bit of ourselves in this kind of behavior."[1]

Similarities between human societies and wildlife populations are not limited to direct stimulus and response. To a great extent, the competition threatening the two groups and their shared habitats results from the same political actions and inactions. In particular, by failing to provide for human populations and population density increases, Kenyan and Tanzanian policy makers have set in motion a devolutionary cycle of increasing densities and declining subsistence for both sets of competitors in their finite commons. All participants lose in this process: people, animals, environment, and, of course, governments.

A linkage of policy problem to policy solution has therefore not emerged at the periphery of human settlement. Subjected to the various pressures of wildlife advocates and neglecting the basic needs of peripheral farmers and herders, the Kenyan policy approach has proved unable to meet goals in either the wildlife or the agricultural sector. The Tanzanian approach has produced identical effects, but for different reasons. In this country the intent was to bring about an immediate transformation of the agricultural periphery, but through resettlement and land-use policies hastily devised and implemented and inadequately supported by the resources on hand. Although neither policy process has achieved an optimal balance of effective wildlife management and meaningful agricultural reform, each government seems likely to proceed with only incremental changes in past assumptions and goal orientations. Current directions should be assessed, however, so that new means can be suggested through which policies might be made to work.

The Kenyan Neglect of Periphery Agriculture

International wildlife organizations have made Kenya their African home, and the country's tourist industry has profited accordingly. Neither interest could hope for better publicity than the sort conveyed by a visiting Canadian journalist:

> Driving...from Nairobi toward the Indian Ocean, there are a
> first-class highway and a railway passenger service passing

through the Tsavo National Park, which has some of the best elephant viewing around. You can drink sundowners on the veranda of the Voi Safari Lodge and feel shivers down your spine when a large bull elephant trumpets from the waterhole out front.[2]

This eulogy fails to mention the large number of elephants that die every year from overcrowding in the park. It also ignores the hardships African societies endure in Tsavo's dry natural environment. These peoples and animals like the elephants bear the brunt of Kenya's worsening imbalances in population growth and food availability.

In the future, Kenya's demographic prospects appear to be even more ominous than Tanzania's. The crude birth rate remained at about 55 per thousand between 1960 and 1982, while the crude death rate fell from 24 to 12 per thousand—a decline of 50 percent.[3] Population growth reflects these trends in fertility and mortality. The total number of Kenyans increased at an average rate of 3.2 percent during the 1960s, and at a rate of 4.0 percent between 1970 and 1982. The World Bank currently projects an annual 4.4 percent average growth rate until the end of the century, tying Kenya with Zimbabwe as the world's fastest growing population.[4]

Gross population distributions must also be considered. Urban populations increased at an average annual rate of over 7 percent from 1970 to 1982, up from the 6.4 percent Kenya experienced between 1960 and 1970. Doubling in less than a generation, this surging population of non-food producers requires a level of subsistence not easily obtained from domestic production or from purchased imports.

Marketed grain yields rose by only 2 percent between 1969–1971 and 1979–1981. Cereal imports expanded from 15,000 tons in 1974 to 194,000 tons in 1982. Because of an external public debt that mushroomed from $688 million (22.2 percent of GNP) in 1976 to $2.36 billion (39.2 percent of GNP) by 1982, the tonnage of cereal grains imported as food aid increased from 2,000 in 1974/1975 to 115,000 in 1981/1982. These subsidies were not enough to make up for an average food production index that dropped from 100 in 1969–1971 to 88 in 1980–1982. Kenyans had access to an average daily per capita food supply of 2,056 calories during 1981, which satisfied only 88 percent of their requirements.[5] In a country where about 80 percent of the national wealth

4.1 Tourism and environmental stress, Tsavo National Park. David Keith Jones.

is consumed by the richest 40 percent of society, and where the poorest 40 percent receives barely 9 percent of the national income, it is not difficult to determine where food shortages are mostly felt—among the urban unemployed and in that part of the peasantry that competes at the agricultural periphery with Kenya's wildlife.

Kenyan versions of state-managed capitalism, unbalanced economic growth, and political elitism have combined to retard agricultural development and to freeze it in those areas not in the fertile highlands. From his study of agricultural extension in the relatively fertile Western Province, David Leonard concluded that

> there is a substantial bias in the distribution of agricultural extension services in Western Kenya, in favor of the wealthier and more progressive farmers. This favoritism accentuates rural inequality and probably prevents the maximum possible acceptance of agricultural innovations. . . . Although the skew in services does not even make good economic sense, it is consistent with the general pattern of benefit distribution in the Kenyan political system. Decision makers probably will not feel any urgency about ameliorating the imbalance in extension until poor farmers emerge as a distinct and noticeable political force and are able to campaign for their own rights.[6]

From the isolation of their deteriorating ecosystems, Kenya's poorest farmers are scarcely better able than wildlife to aggregate their concerns. What the peasants lack, however, game animals possess—an active lobby in Nairobi that effectively speaks on behalf of wildlife interests. Adding to the poignancy of this situation is a continuing series of droughts in locations that include most of the country's wildlife areas. The latest drought began in 1983 and by late 1984 had become the worst in fifty years of Kenyan history. A 45 percent production loss was projected for the staple crop maize, and deaths related to malnutrition and undernutrition were increasingly reported in the arid, northern two-thirds of the country.

Research suggests that "reaching the peasant farmer" is a problem throughout modern Kenya. In his 1973 analysis of agricultural land reform in the central highlands, John Harbison discovered a failure of communication also prevalent in the more remote areas, where wildlife advocates concentrate their attention and where official development policy has had even less impact.

It is clear that decision-makers and administrators have not established rapport with the intended participants in the developing modern economy. Central government planners and decision-makers have no channels they consider reliable for understanding the problems of grass-roots participants, for distinguishing between legitimate and illegitimate complaints by them, or for establishing any kind of dialogue with them in order to resolve outstanding issues. Decision-makers decide and participants respond largely in ignorance of each other's intentions and points of view. When the grass-roots participants have only rudimentary knowledge of the economic structure into which they are being initiated, this lack of rapport can seriously undermine their positive response to the structure of incentives and admonitions which central government planners try to establish.[7]

Livestock, currently accounting for 30 percent of Kenyan agricultural output and for about 9 percent of all exports, represent the most attractive economic structure in the northern and eastern parts of the country and in selected regions of the southwest. Nevertheless, little effective emphasis has yet been placed on livestock in these peripheral expanses of light population density but also of low rainfall and extremely delicate environmental equilibria. Most Kenyan pastoralists are seminomadic Sudanic and Cushitic speakers, culturally and physically isolated from the elites in power. For the government, the central policy issue is how to enhance these pastoralists' participation in the national economy without destroying their ability to survive and without causing them to exterminate game animals as a consequence of their entry into the marketplace. A few ranching schemes have been tried, but these have not been well financed, planned, or implemented and have fallen easy victim to drought and overgrazing.

Rural development officers and wildlife advocates agree that the free-roaming lifestyles of Kenya's pastoral communities should be curtailed. Although these groups have not been provided with acceptable land-use alternatives, outsiders still complain they are economically noncontributive, difficult to assist, environmentally disruptive, prone to internecine violence, and generally impossible to govern. Like its general problems of satisfying wildlife interests while balancing population growth and food availability, Kenya's pastoral dilemma is both economic and political.

In an atmosphere of rural hardship and withdrawal, of lengthening food lines and mounting urban unrest, and of international pauperization and dependency, it is difficult to imagine how the Kenyan wildlife and land-use situations can be improved until basic reforms are undertaken across the entire range of policy-making and administrative functions, from informed goal selection to dispassionate performance evaluation. Human needs and available resources do not coincide in modern Kenya, yet they must be aligned if the ecology's three components are to survive—people, wildlife, and the environment that supports them.

The Kenyan environment demands the utmost in ecological stewardship. Areas north of the central and western highlands are characterized by a very dry climate and by vast stretches of scrubland interspersed with rocky outcrops and mountains. Pastoralists share this space with scattered herds of wild ungulates and have always competed with them for water and land. Both groups are now reaching their limits as the grazing commons nears exhaustion, as human populations continue to grow, and as wild animals are increasingly exposed to poaching for profit and food. To the south of the highlands lies a normally well-watered savanna that contains abundant wildlife, exploding African populations, and in the drier eastern portion Kenya's largest national park. Here too the mutual fight for survival is intensifying as the environment is rendered insufficient for sustaining the situation. In the south, soil depletion and erosion have exacerbated land shortages. Erosion has reached such proportions that hydroelectric stations are frequently incapacitated by soil run-off and silting.

Set against these realities are the wildlife establishment and the tourist industry. Tourism increased significantly after independence and by 1972 accounted for more than 40,000 jobs, nearly half of all positions provided by manufacturing activities. By 1981, a total of 22,000 hotel beds were available in Kenya, as compared with less than 6,000 in 1965. Of about 362,000 foreign visitors in 1980, some 282,000 came on vacations from Europe, North America, and Japan. Their spending generated over $20 million in foreign exchange.[8]

Although the long-term prospects may be good for Kenyan tourism, several problems presently affect the industry. Tourism is very sensitive to prevailing economic conditions, and business fell off considerably during the international recession of 1979-1981. Moreover, because most airline and hotel reservations are made outside Kenya, a sizeable share of total revenues never enters the national economy. In trying to recoup some of these losses, the Kenyan government imposed fees on visas and charter carriers, an act that further contributed to an estimated 15 percent decline in tourist visits between 1980 and 1981. The 1982 military uprising prevented the industry from taking early advantage of a recovering international economy.[9]

Social and developmental costs are also associated with tourism. Racially and culturally distinct vacationers demand expensive imported commodities and tend to engage in ostentatious displays of affluence that, to many Kenyans, raise serious questions of inequity and neocolonialism. Another issue concerns the actual economic benefits bestowed by foreign visitors. Some analysts have suggested that, in light of the infrastructural costs of game lodges, resorts, and transportation services, the sector's direct returns may not exceed 10 percent of gross receipts.[10] Viewed from a short-range perspective, tourism may not be the wisest way to spend scarce foreign exchange when compared with other items such as fuels, fertilizers, and farm equipment.[11]

The official view, however, is one of great enthusiasm for tourism as a generator of development capital. Heavy government spending has been directed at airport improvements and toward the national parks, game reserves, and beach resorts. The parastatal Kenya Tourist Development Corporation has conducted extensive promotional campaigns in Europe, Japan, and North America, and the government has obtained major loans to finance the total Kenyanization of employment in the sector. For the foreseeable future, wildlife-centered tourism will form a primary component of the Kenyan economy. This policy emphasis complements the varied interests of the wildlife protection community, but presents a formidable obstacle to food production and rural development in locations where wildlife populations are better supported than are peasant farmers and herders.

Kenya contains a highly active wildlife advocacy that contrasts with extreme land hunger and relentless territoriality. The central and western highlands serve as the center of food and export crop production. Maize is the region's most important food crop and uses up about 40 percent of all cultivated land. Slightly over 20 percent of Kenyan food consumption is home grown, and the rest must be purchased or obtained in barter

4.2 The price of protection: elephant at Maasi Serena lodge, Masaai Mara National Reserve. David Keith Jones.

trade. This distribution means that rapidly expanding rural and urban populations are heavily dependent on maize output in the highlands.

Domestic maize yields have not met national needs since 1978, when highland farmers began to experience serious overcrowding and, also, began to forsake maize in favor of more profitable export crops. To regain food sufficiency by 1989, the government has projected a 4.9 percent average annual growth in maize production. With the technologies and input levels now in place, 940,000 hectares (2.4 million acres) must be brought under cultivation to meet this requirement. An additional 220,000 hectares (550,000 acres) must be devoted to wheat, sorghum, and millet.[12] The problem is that the easily cultivated highlands are now fully utilized and are increasingly taxed by population pressures resulting in smaller land holdings and in soil depletion and environmental destruction.

The United Nations has acknowledged this dilemma. According to a recent calculation by the Food and Agriculture Organization, in 1975 Kenya's ratio of population-supporting agricultural capacity to actual population density fell to below 1.0.[13] Since that time, the amount of cultivated land has not grown appreciably, but population densities have. Accordingly, FAO has included Kenya with the fourteen tropical African countries that lack sufficient land for subsistence-level agriculture to support populations as large as were attained in 1975.[14] In the past, higher rural densities and food surpluses were sustained in the highlands by the kinds of basic agricultural innovations commonly practiced in Asia and Latin America—notably hybrid seed utilization, irrigation, and double cropping. These solutions have now reached their points of diminishing return. In FAO's estimation, Kenya and six other African countries will not attain food sufficiency by the year 2000 (when the Kenyan population is expected to reach 40 million), "even if their agricultural techniques were to match those now found on commercial farms in Asia and Latin America."[15]

Population pressures threaten the only ecological zones easily adapted to improved farming systems, the highlands, which constitute less than 10 percent of Kenya's land area. Attention must now be focused on the agricultural periphery, which has previously been left to largely unassisted subsistence agriculture and also to wildlife sanctuaries whose revenues could help pay the developmental bill. Yet there is little sign that this effort will be seriously undertaken in the near future. Unless decisive policy interventions *are* made to balance and serve both human and wildlife needs, the conflict between man and animals will continue. As in the wildlife areas of Tanzania, this struggle has gone on since the earliest of times, but it cannot persist for much longer.[16]

The Tanzanian Neglect of Land-Use Reform

Little doubt remains that ecological stresses have reached crisis levels in modern Tanzania and that a significant part of these problems involves faulty agricultural land-use strategies. It is also clear that, in the official Tanzanian view, any effort to restore ecological harmony must begin with an attempt to square food availability with population growth and distribution. A rapidly growing Tanzanian population is matched by an average per capita food supply of less than 2,000 daily calories, which meets only about 83 percent of minimum requirements. More than half these calories typically consist of complex carbohydrates, deficient in fats, sugars, and proteins. The dynamics of population growth guarantee that, unless agricultural productivity is quickly and permanently increased, undernutrition and malnutrition will envelop society as the Tanzanian environment approaches physical exhaustion. Neither land users nor egalitarian development strategies can long endure these conditions.

Tanzania's crude annual birth rate stood at 47 per thousand between 1960 and 1982, but the crude death rate dropped by 31.8 percent during the same period, from 22 to 15 per thousand annually. Food supplies must expand exponentially to keep pace with a population growth rate of about 3.4 percent and with a yearly urban growth rate of nearly 9 percent.[17] Most of this food will have to come from internal production, since Tanzania simply cannot afford large-scale grain imports. The external public debt rose from $248 million (19.4 percent of GNP) in 1970 to nearly $1.7 billion (32.7 percent of GNP) by 1982.[18] These increases have occurred in spite of rigidly curtailed imports, including fertilizers and fuels.

Although not as severe as in Kenya, Tanzania's population outlook is worsened by the country's inability to feed itself. In Kenya, marketed grain output grew slightly between 1969–1971 and 1979–1981, from 1.47

to 1.50 tons per hectare. In Tanzania, marketed grain yields actually fell during the same period, from 0.78 to 0.70 tons per hectare.[19] This absolute decrease in an already marginal level of grain production resulted largely from two factors. Unfavorable producer prices and other economic disincentives discouraged peasants from growing food surpluses and encouraged them to sell any excess on the black market where prices are higher and no records are kept. In addition, villagization and its officially mandated but technically unsupported intensification of agriculture led to widespread erosion and loss of soil fertility.

The Tanzanian economic policy problem, also encountered in Kenya, is discussed elsewhere.[20] The present focus is on recent trends in land use and their implications for Tanzanian wildlife. Here, the most likely policy alternatives favor not programs to reduce population growth, but rather land-tenure rules and technoeconomic services that are sensitive to existing local capabilities in Tanzania's varied ecological settings.[21] If such improvements can be made, agricultural productivity will increase through intensification of land use. As a supplementary benefit, wildlife will be protected so that preservation, conservation, and utilization objectives can be set for them.

Writing in 1980, Ergas identified five erroneous assumptions of the villagization-based, agricultural strategy of the late 1960s and 1970s.

1. That peasants will freely and universally communalize their land holdings
2. That capitalist farming enterprises, featuring individual ownership and private decision making, do not provide powerful models for peasants to emulate
3. That mass participation in rural development projects can be easily secured
4. That party and government bureaucrats are heavily committed to rural development and to building a socialist society
5. That peasants can be expected to be completely self-reliant and, at the same time, to produce surplus food and export crops.[22]

The first two fallacies influenced an unsuccessful attempt to communalize ownership of the land and its produce, and the remaining misconceptions prompted a serious underestimation of the assistance needed to transform subsistence cultivators into self-sustaining *and* income-seeking agribusinessmen. Subsequent administrative, economic, and political failures have persuaded the elite to postpone the transition to rural socialism and self-reliance and to modify the means selected to activate the rural sector.

Full-scale communalization was legislatively abandoned in 1975, even as the villagization campaign was entering its final phase. The *Chama Cha Mapinduzi* (Revolutionary Party) guidelines, revised in 1981, reaffirm the national commitment to rural socialism, a pledge repeated by President Nyerere in his keynote address to the Second Ordinary Conference of the party in October 1982.[23] Nevertheless, the general unwillingness of peasants to collectivize their farming plots has since forced policy makers to permit private cultivation on individual holdings grouped into farming blocks. Cooperative societies were reintroduced in 1982 to maximize productive incentives and capacities. Producers' cooperatives had been banned in 1975–1976 because they were judged to be corrupt and biased in favor of already more prosperous, cash-crop farmers.

Important as they are, such incentives cannot serve as panaceas. Tanzanian peasants clearly prefer the security of individual tenure, but are willing and able to produce surpluses only if approached with more numerous and effective agricultural inputs and services. Cooperative societies can create economies of scale, but unless they are supported on a nationwide basis in food as well as export crops, they will also promote inequality and the growth of a rural underclass in the less arable and overcrowded parts of the country—precisely the locations of the most pressing rural food and land-use problems. A planned and managed communalization of agriculture, requiring closely controlled and equalized incomes, is more in keeping with Tanzanian policy goals. But to allay the peasantry's aversion to an equalization of poverty, this choice would necessitate far more developmental assistance than is now within reach.

What the 1981 party guidelines praise as "big socialist farms" could worsen Tanzania's chronic difficulties with large and inefficient bureaucracies in the governmental and parastatal sectors. They could also completely destroy what is left of individual incentives and official market participation by farm workers. These results will occur unless policies can be introduced that will improve producer prices and upgrade agricultural research, extension, credit, and productive inputs. Vastly improved marketing, transport, and storage services are also required. Technical and economic innovations are critical to the success of whatever developmental strategy is finally adopted. They are equally crucial to environmental and wildlife protection and, indeed, to national political integration and social harmony.

Recent policy trends bear mixed implications for agricultural land-use and wildlife concerns. Adequate food supplies and sufficient foreign exchange to cover necessary imports constitute Tanzania's most immediate economic challenges. A viable wildlife policy depends on solutions to the first problem, but it can help resolve the second. Simply stated, food sufficiency will reduce pressures on the wildlife areas so that tourism, a major potential source of foreign exchange, can be promoted. It is not yet clear whether this planned sequence is about to begin.

In April 1983, the party-government announced that the agricultural share of the development budget would be raised from 13 to 23 percent. The lion's share of this increase, however, was directed toward export crops. During the same month, a $50 million agreement was concluded with the Aga Khan Secretariat based in France. The money was intended to help rehabilitate the tourist industry and was soon followed by additional foreign investments for this purpose. On the other hand, the Ministry of Agriculture has reported that soil erosion and desertification may already have reached unmanageable proportions in parts of Mwanza, Shinyanga, Mara, Arusha, Singida, and Dodoma regions. All but Singida and Dodoma include or adjoin the northern game parks, which attract the largest number of tourists.

At the village level, the new party guidelines exhort the leadership toward basic-needs satisfaction in food.[24] Previously dispersed among the various regional authorities, the agricultural extension service has again been consolidated into the Ministry of Agriculture. The ministry has followed suit by emphasizing extension, particularly field demonstrations of recommended cultivation and conservation methods. By October 1982, the president was also able to report that nearly all villages contained primary schools, that 90 percent had cooperative shops, and that 30 percent enjoyed easy access to rural medical facilities.[25] He also pointed to shortages of teachers and teaching materials, to a grain collection and transportation system that remained in a state of virtual collapse, and to woefully inadequate village technologies that neglected basic innovations such as small-scale irrigation and soil conservation. These deficiencies have worsened in more recent years.

Although Tanzania's balance-of-payments deficit approached $300 million by the mid-1980s, much of the responsibility for these lapses must be assigned to the size, cost, and elitist pretentions of the political class of managers and bureaucratic functionaries.[26] Civil service employment was reduced by 10 percent in 1976, but has since risen by 35 percent when teachers are excluded. Wages and salaries consume about 66 percent of recurrent regional budgets, which must also help fund rural development projects. In an example drawn from the wildlife sector, the president observed that "the anti-poaching campaigns in the National Parks are conducted by increasing the number of people in Headquarters and Divisional Offices while failing to renew the vehicles given to us only a few years ago."[27] On the food crop front, the number of diploma-level extension officers increased from 739 in 1972 to 1,795 by 1982, and the contingent of degree holders grew from 232 to 758. To explain diminishing per capita food availability, Nyerere was forced to conclude that "quite clearly, either our training is wrongly directed or our Agricultural Extension Officers are not doing what they are expected to do." Further,

> we set "targets" for different crops, usually starting at the central Government level and working downwards. We have arranged "cash crops" for areas which did not have a high-earner traditionally. We have negotiated "Maize Projects" and "Tobacco Projects" with international agencies. And so on. Yet I say now that we have neglected agriculture.[28]

President Nyerere has also pointed out that in spite of a persistent foreign exchange crisis, relatively inexpensive innovations can now be applied to intensify food production, to create incentives for food crop producers, and to protect the environment. In addition to higher producer prices, these measures include the promotion of crop rotation, composting, fertilization with manure, and intercropping under appropriate soil and moisture conditions. Improved farm implements are also necessary and affordable, especially those employing animal traction. Labor-intensive irrigation and reforestation projects should also be mentioned, but, as Nyerere lamented, "when have we, as political leaders, or when have our Bwana Shamba [extension officers] demonstrated these points and taught their meaning and their significance? How can output fail to go down?"[29]

An Implementation Secretariat has been established in the Ministry of Economic Affairs and Development Planning, with jurisdiction over the other ministries, the regional administrations, and the parastatal corporations. One of its duties is to enforce the president's prime directive for the latter 1980s: "We have enough land to allow every able bodied Tanzanian to participate in the production of food *and* cash crops. For I stress, no-one in this country has a right to wage-employment. What we do have a right to is an opportunity to work. That opportunity exists. It exists on our land."[30]

In a further move to fulfill this mandate, in late 1984 the Morogoro agricultural campus of the University of Dar es Salaam was converted into the Sokoine University of Agriculture (named after the prime minister who earlier that year was killed in a road accident). In his address at its inauguration ceremonies, President Nyerere outlined the university's revised goals in teaching, research, and public service.

4.3 Leadership by example: President Nyerere (hoe raised) clearing bush near his home village of Butiama, Mara Region.

The emphasis must be on practical development. And this requires new departures in Tanzanian education. For until now we have no tradition or experience of training farmers. The Faculty of Agriculture, Forestry and Veterinary Science of the University of Dar es Salaam did not train farmers. And the various Ministry of Agriculture Training Institutions did not do so. All have been training future Civil Servants, and awarding them Degrees, Diplomas or Certificates. Now I am asking this University to rescue us from the absurdity of an agricultural country which has no institutions where people can learn to be farmers, or better farmers. Some of the people you train will still become Civil Servants in the future, and will require the necessary qualifications. But your real purpose is to help us in the training of farmers, and in the education and training of experts who are both capable of training practical farmers and willing to do so.[31]

These openings, one may correctly infer, are the first and foremost developmental options available to the Tanzanian society. But if aggressive exploitation of the land is *not* accompanied by knowledgeable and cost-effectively managed supports and by a balanced combination of discipline and inducement, it will exacerbate existing food and population disequilibria and thereby hasten ecological, economic, and political collapse in the countryside and in the urban areas as well.

If future policy endeavors fall short and if expanding and impoverished communities are driven into Tanzania's agricultural "last places on earth," then already endangered wildlife species will become extinct. Current wildlife policy reflects an uncertain tendency toward the preservation of game animals and their habitats, with some concern expressed for conservation through culling supposedly overpopulated herds. Game utilization for meat production is frequently discussed but has not yet been attempted on a commercial scale. Continued failure of agricultural land-use policy will resolve this ambiguity by eliminating the need to choose between preservation, conservation, and utilization alternatives. It will also mean that Tanzania has abandoned its scientific and moral obligation to protect one of Africa's last genetic pools of disappearing species, that all hope for a profitable tourist industry must be forsaken, and that the tempting notion of wild ungulates as an immense source of food protein will forever remain chimerical.

As in Kenya, none of Tanzania's issues of land use and wildlife can be ignored, and each must be approached in relation to the others. Julius

Nyerere has often reminded the nation that "we have to make choices between good things, not between good things and bad things: to plan
means to choose." So that past mistakes and omissions can be avoided,
Kenyan and Tanzanian policy choices must cease to be dominated by political expediencies and ideological rigidities. This rather large task in
turn requires a constant flow of applied research and considerable elite-
mass cooperation in the political and administrative spheres.

Requirements for the Policy Process

For substantive reforms to be undertaken in Kenyan and Tanzanian rural
development policy, the policy situation in each country must itself be re-
vamped. Here the most basic problems have to do with improving the
knowledge base and performance of politicians, administrators, and land
users. Before addressing these needs, it should first be noted that their
fulfillment must primarily result from self-interested domestic initiatives.
Little bilateral or multilateral development assistance supports land-use
reforms that also protect wildlife. The same can be said about the work
of private wildlife associations and other voluntary organizations. Their
offerings are also small and uncoordinated and, in the case of wildlife
groups, are directed more toward protecting endangered species than toward correcting the human causes of wildlife endangerment. In short,
whatever steps are taken to alleviate the conditions discussed in preceding chapters must largely be taken by informed domestic policy makers
with the needed resources at their command. Tourist revenues may help
in this effort, if tourism is revived in Tanzania[32] and its profits reoriented
in Kenya, but most other foreign monies are either committed to wildlife
preservation or preoccupied with raising agricultural production and the
international prestige of aid donors. With its dearth of important background information and its hidden political agendas, moreover, external
assistance can even work at cross-purposes to better land use.[33]

    Eastern Africa's rural dilemmas have stimulated a large outpouring
of recent research.[34] Nevertheless, scant attention has yet been paid to the
demographics and techniques of agrarian land use in relation to the vast
expanses legally reserved for wildlife. As Eicher has pointed out, applied
research is a vital component of long-term solutions to Africa's agricul-

tural problems.[35] It is also essential to any reduction in the growing struggle over the agricultural peripheries of Tanzania and Kenya. In no small
measure, this conflict results from policy goals and programs that are uninformed and therefore counterproductive for agriculturalists and wildlife alike.

RESEARCH REQUIREMENTS

From the perspective of the national parks, reserves, and controlled areas, a series of detailed studies is needed on the interactions of wild animals with their own and other species, with their physical environments,
and with man. In particular, human interventions to preserve, conserve,
and utilize wildlife should be based on a much fuller body of knowledge
than presently exists. Norton-Griffiths underlines this prerequisite in reference to scientifically ill-advised conservation efforts in the Serengeti
and Tsavo National Parks.

> It is unfortunate that the conservation "ethic" is so often couched
> in terms of maintaining the existing diversity of plant and animal
> life, for ecologically this is a contradiction in terms and is
> unsuitable for highly dynamic and highly unstable ecosystems.
> Such a goal might be attainable in mesic, climax communities,
> such as rain forests, but it is unrealistic (with our existing
> knowledge) for areas that experience either random climatic
> perturbations (Serengeti) or cyclical climatic perturbations
> (Tsavo). Stability has no place in systems such as these.[36]

At the point of contact between human and wildlife populations—
also the point of interception between agricultural land-use and wildlife
policies—the need for data is especially acute. In his study of livestock
development and the potential for game utilization in Kenya, Davis identified an even wider informational gap in Tanzania. Davis' analysis suggested the likelihood that "projections of livestock development may
have gone beyond the point of optimal development . . . and that with
further development of the wildlife industries, opportunities will arise to
substitute wildlife enterprises for livestock at the margin. But in the absence of a major research and development effort, the wildlife herds may
slip into oblivion with the question never having been answered."[37]

In the east central Selous, Matzke discovered that the presence of

Tanzanian farming communities inhibited certain indigenous species but had little effect on others.[38] From this finding, Matzke recommended that "because of its manageability, serious consideration of the wildlife/settlement interface is an appropriate endeavor for individuals concerned with minimizing the problems of agricultural vermin, and/or maximizing the benefits of the Tanzanian wildlife resources."[39] Matzke's research design should be applied in other parts of the Selous and its results tested elsewhere in eastern Africa.

From the standpoint of agricultural land use in the human-wildlife nexus, the most critical need is for reliable data on food, nutrition, demographics, and economic conditions in the rural areas, especially at the agricultural periphery. In Tanzania, for example, the last major study of food availabilities and nutritional statuses was completed in 1978,[40] but it contains only regional data and says nothing about districts and villages. Although census data are better now than in the past, they are only collected at ten-year intervals. The Tanzanian Ministry of Agriculture produces food production estimates from questionnaire returns from regional agricultural development officers, but the ministry expresses little confidence in this monitoring system, considering it "not objective and hence not very reliable."[41] The University of Dar es Salaam has only recently revived a series of village economic input-output surveys, a project cancelled in the first years after independence because of its expense and because of a research staff requirement that could not be met. In both Tanzania and Kenya, a lack of local background information prevents accurate assessments of actual pressures on the land and thus precludes the recommendation of effective countermeasures.

Beyond these introductory probes, precise determinations must be made of the technical and environmental aspects of existing agricultural practices. These case studies will help decision makers ascertain which self-supporting and surplus-producing agricultural systems are also ecologically sensitive and environmentally protective. Since they reside in semiarid locations (which helps explain their proximity to the largest wildlife areas), most of the Kenyan and Tanzanian target populations are committed to dryland cultivation and pastoralism. At present, they provide no exception to Eicher's generalization about "the lack of proven technical packages for small farmers in dry land farming systems throughout Africa, and the uniformly unfavorable technical coefficients (e.g., low rates of growth, disease) for livestock production."[42] In better-watered environments, recent West African experiments in agroforestry, where fast-growing leguminous trees were interplanted with crops, may prove applicable. The trees promoted agricultural intensification by fixing nitrogen and by producing a rich organic mulch. They also reduced erosion and offered a ready supply of fuelwood.[43] But even in these more humid ecosystems, such as in Tanzania's Kilimanjaro Region and in the Aberdare and Mt. Kenya areas of Kenya, the specific types and limits of intensification must be carefully established. From his study of Chagga land use, Maro concluded that

> there is need for more research in Kilimanjaro, especially to assess accurately the capacity of the soils and rainfall regime to support a variety of crops, and to establish accurate production figures for kitchen gardens and all crops. Information on these topics could be obtained through micro-study of sample areas for a period of not less than five years. Such studies would enable planners to determine the extent to which intensification in agriculture should be carried.[44]

Incentives and other behavioral factors must also be addressed in land-use research, even though they raise some of the most complicated and politically sensitive issues. As Ndissi recommended in his study of Iringa Rural District, minimally acceptable levels of productive investment will have to be squared with the desired levels of social overhead expenditure in the village settings of each Tanzanian locality. Productively optimal land-tenure and working arrangements, which reconcile peasant interests with the egalitarian objectives of the national leadership, will likewise have to be devised and implemented.[45] In Kenya, less intrusive policies must be applied that reflect this country's capitalistic approaches to investment, employment, property, and income.

Research is a necessary but insufficient condition for agricultural development and wildlife protection. In both Kenya and Tanzania, land-use innovations require delivery systems as closely tied to applied research programs as are American cooperative extension services to agricultural experiment stations. Properly adjusted to the economic constraints and sociopolitical milieus of each country, this model of closely coordinated research and extension can assist farmers in raising improved food and export crops on well-managed agricultural holdings. Humans and wildlife will profit from the resulting fusion of knowledge and action, but only if politicians and administrators enhance their capacity to reach peasant farmers and if peasant farmers are themselves permitted some say in the obligations they are asked to bear.[46]

ELITE AND MASS INVOLVEMENT

International development agencies have generally concluded that Africa's human ecological problems are too great to be resolved by Africans. Accordingly, the World Bank has advocated a "new kind of social compact, an agreement within the world community that the struggle against poverty in Africa is a joint concern which entails responsibilities for both parties,"[47] aid doners and aid recipients. For its part, the United States government allocated about $75 million of its $1.1 billion 1985 African aid budget to the first phase of an "African Economic Policy Initiative." This program seeks to provide "tangible support for countries prepared to undertake the difficult policy reforms needed to improve productivity, especially in agriculture, and provide farmers incentives to produce more food."[48] To qualify for support, African governments must encourage private enterprise and be willing to admit foreign investment capital "to expand the food production base."

Overtures of this kind reflect a growing international recognition of tropical Africa's present ecological crisis and the need for reforms in leadership; but, as suggested earlier, they offer no substitutes for purely African efforts and can, indeed, thwart these endeavors. The Economic Policy Initiative demonstrates that aid programs embody the ideological preferences of their donors, which may or may not coincide with the policy constraints and goals of recipient governments. Further, the actual distribution of assistance often coincides with big-power policy objectives that are irrelevant to Africa's developmental needs and can retard their fulfillment. In eastern Africa, Kenya has become a strategically important ally of the United States; Tanzania has not. The United States' relationship with Kenya was strengthened in the initial three years of the first Reagan administration, but Tanzania experienced a steady decline in American development assistance. At much higher levels, development aid to Kenya remained relatively steady during the same period, but security and military assistance increased by 80 percent. Table 4.1 quantifies these trends which have more recently culminated in fiscal 1986 aid budgets of $97 million for Kenya but only $1.4 million for Tanzania.

Table 4.1.   United States Aid Funding to Kenya and Tanzania, 1981–1984

| Category/Fiscal Year[a] | ($ thousand in rounded current dollars) | | | |
	Kenya	%	Tanzania	%
Food and Development[b]				
1981 (Carter)	44,340	79	36,290	100
1982 (Reagan)	46,300	51	18,250	100
1983 (Reagan)	48,800	42	18,000	99
1984 (Reagan)	47,000	37	14,000	99
Security and Military[c]				
1981 (Carter)	12,020	21	-	00
1982 (Reagan)	43,800	49	-	00
1983 (Reagan)	66,400	58	80	01
1984 (Reagan)	78,650	63	75	01

[a]Figures for 1981 and 1982 are actual estimated expenditures; figures for 1983 and 1984 represent planning levels.
[b]P.L. 480 Food Sales and Grants, Development Assistance.
[c]Economic Support Fund, Military Credit Sales, Military Assistance Program, International Military Education and Training.
SOURCES: U.S. Agency for International Development, *Congressional Presentation, Fiscal Year 1982*, main volume (amended version) (Washington: U.S. International Development Cooperation Agency, n.d.), pp. 452–453; U.S.A.I.D., *Congressional Presentation, Fiscal Year 1983*, main volume (n.d.), pp 481, 488, 495; and U.S. Congress, *Foreign Assistance Legislation for Fiscal Years 1984–1985*, part 8 (Washington: Subcommittee on Africa, House Committee on Foreign Affairs, 98th Congress, first session, March-April 1983), pp. 95–96.

In neither situation is a heavy reliance on foreign aid conducive to resolving the issues discussed in this volume. In the Tanzanian case, year-to-year funding reductions were partly caused by philosophic and operational differences between donor and recipient as to the nature and purposes of development. These disagreements and their consequences have further lessened the effectiveness of projects that may have been ill-conceived in the first place and, in any case, have already consumed large amounts of Tanzania's scarce domestic resources. For Kenya, the implications of aid dependency are even more problematic. A locally dominant assistance program that spends more for coercive capability than for development is bound to have a destabilizing effect on a regime that has become a political and military client of a big power. The Kenyan air force received the bulk of United States military assistance during the early 1980s, and elements within this branch were those responsible for the aborted coup of 1982.[49] With their narrow and self-serving agendas to pursue, large contingents of foreign investors and wildlife advocates have only added to the confusion of goal selection in a policy system deeply penetrated by external interests.

Although international technical and financial resources can play an important facilitative role,[50] solutions to African development problems will have to be initiated and carried out by Africans. In the immediate contexts of Kenya and Tanzania, food sufficiency and ecological harmony can only result from the enlightened self-interests, domestic resource contributions, and joint hard work of both countries' elites and masses. The major challenge in both policy arenas centers on how best to promote these realizations and commitments. The objects of such attentions must be well-integrated improvements across the entire range of land-use conditions created by man and other species.

In a recent issue of its journal, the public interest group Resources for the Future offered the following assessment of the current world food situation:

> Detailed examination of land and water resources and of the possibilities of raising yields by increased applications of inputs and technology suggests that all regions will meet increased demand largely out of domestic production. While the rates of growth of demand are particularly high in some developing regions, these generally also are the regions where production technology has been lagging and the potential for productivity growth is, therefore, very large. Realizing this potential will require massive investments in land improvement, irrigation, research, and extension; adequate inputs of fertilizer, pesticides, and improved seeds; improved marketing and storage facilities; and adequate economic incentives.[51]

The world's fastest growing demand for domestic food production and also its greatest potential for productivity growth lie in Africa. In addition to inadequate research findings and insufficient investment capital, what Africa lacks is the necessary political leadership to facilitate permanent increases in food availability. In different ways, Kenya and Tanzania share this deficiency. They also share an asset in wildlife that, if accommodated in research and in land-use policy, can lessen the financial burden of agricultural and rural development. The research question has been addressed. This study concludes with some final observations on the two countries' leadership requirements and financial opportunities in land-use and wildlife policy.

To a very large degree, relations between African leadership groups and the masses of African peasants are as ships passing in the night. Neither side is able to deal effectively with the other, and each side receives little perceived benefit from joint problem-solving endeavors. With the help of Jackson and Rosberg, the elite side of these incompatibilities was presented in the preface to this volume. In his latest and most important commentary on the subject, Goran Hyden explains some of the problem's root causes from the peasant perspective.

> As the productive and reproductive needs of the peasants can be met without the support of other social classes, relations between those who rule and those who till the land are not firmly rooted in the production system as such. Instead, appropriations by those in control of the state are made in the form of taxation and as such they are simple deductions from an already produced stock of values. These are tributary rather than productive relations and they do imply a much more limited degree of social control. In this respect, African countries are societies without a state. The latter sits suspended in "mid-air" over the society and is not an integral mechanism of the day-to-day productive activities of society.[52]

Under these circumstances, government is mainly conducted through unstable patronage interactions, punctuated by sporadic attempts to force compliance with unpopular policy decisions. Both techniques preclude planned policy responses to issues of great public moment.

This crisis of political communication is most felt where peasants' productive and reproductive needs can no longer be satisfied without official support, where challenges to human survival have now reached crisis proportions—in the isolated homesteads, sedentary villages, and mobile camps dotting the agricultural periphery and surrounding the legally designated wildlife sanctuaries. Physically and participatively, these communities are the farthest removed from the Kenyan and Tanzanian systems of production, reward, and control. Their problems also tend to be far removed in the minds of Kenyan and Tanzanian policy elites, who are preoccupied with more immediate issues arising in the politically unstable commercial farming areas, towns, and cities. In short, lapses in leadership are even greater at the interface of land-use and wild-life policy than in the broader policy arena to which Hyden refers.

The Kenyan leadership dilemma is further complicated by the world's highest population growth rate, combined with the fact that less than 20 percent of the land is arable. Together, these factors have produced densities that exceed carrying capacities, terminal fragmentations of land holdings, and epidemic landlessness and out-migration in the well-watered highlands. The same imbalances have led to an explosion of new settlements in marshy, semiarid, and arid locations unsuited to low-technology argiculture. For a country in which nearly 50 percent of the formal, wage-earning work force depends on public sector employment, these trends portend political disaster. In a generally optimistic review of the late 1960s and early 1970s, Bienen warned that "if population continues to grow at high rates, Kenya's arable land cannot be encroached on indefinitely. Opening up new land is costly and capital-consuming because it frequently requires draining or irrigation. Thus the future is hardly one to be sanguine about from the point of view of a regime that is sensitive to and responsive to peasant demands and has real roots and political support in the countryside."[53] Since Bienen wrote, these roots and political supports have eroded in direct proportion to the rapid growth of an urbanized bureaucratic elite increasingly isolated from the rest of society and to a steady worsening of the ecological dislocations gripping the rural areas. The policy system remains, in Hyden's simile, "a state with no structural roots in society which, as a balloon suspended in mid-air, is being punctured by excessive demands and unable to function without an indiscriminate and wasteful consumption of scarce societal resources."[54]

Structurally and functionally, the Kenyatta and Moi regimes have progressively expanded and centralized the developmental role of government yet have failed to encourage local self-help activities through centrally provided resources and incentives. In a throwback to the colonial period, the country's forty nonurban districts are still headed by presidentially appointed commissioners and are grouped into seven rural provinces also dominated by the central administration. This concentration of power at the top is inevitably embodied in the design and implementation of rural development projects, such as the Special Rural Development Programme discussed in chapter 3. As Hyden has observed, "where bureaucracy prevails over the market. . .there is little challenge to existing pre-capitalist values and as they tend to survive, the scope for development remains extremely limited."[55]

From his case study of capitalism, political elitism, and their ecological consequences in modern Kenya, William Murdoch was forced to conclude the following:

> The independent Kenyan government since 1964 has simply extended [colonial] policies by "Africanizing" previously white areas without altering the basic policy of concentrating development on a restricted land-owning class in the areas with high-potential farmland. Thus a continuing stream of landless migrants has been forced to leave high-potential areas, which receive almost all the government investment in agriculture. These migrants exert ever-greater pressure on the marginal area of the [central] Plateau, which has received virtually no investment to help deal with this influx. In the meantime, land farther east has been accumulated by large commercial enterprises involved in ranching, tourism, irrigated horticulture for export, and the stripping of scrubland to produce charcoal for export. The displaced dryland farmers are thus pushed westward toward ecologically vulnerable land that they must inevitably overexploit.[56]

Essentially the same fate has overtaken many of Tanzania's marginal rural areas, but under quite different ideological circumstances and as a result of an egalitarian rather than an elitist approach to development policy. The effect of these differences has been a more uniform distribution of the environmental depredations Murdoch encountered to the north. As in Kenya, however, these tragedies of the commons relate to serious failures in communication between leaders and peasants, and today they threaten the inhabitants of every Tanzanian wildlife area.

As part of an effort to equalize resource allocation among Tanzania's twenty mainland regions, the government administration was decentralized in 1972. The goal was to increase the policy-making autonomy of local bureaucrats and party officials and not to promote popular participation in the development process. Under the decentralization plan, existing local government structures were abolished. These structures included partly elected district councils that had served important agenda-setting and managerial purposes by aggregating the expressed needs of rural communities and by sorting out those needs that could be

serviced with local tax revenues and/or through peasant self-help. Decentralization devolved programmatic responsibilities and personnel
from the sectoral ministries to a newly formed prime minister's office,
and concentrated developmental functions into the hands of regional
commissioners employed by the prime minister.

Even more than the loss of economic self-determination caused by
the dissolution of cooperatives, these broadly based political changes
weakened the role of farmers in rural development. They strengthened
the control of administrators and, less directly, local party officers who
were intended to provide ideological guidance in the selection and implementation of development projects. The new arrangements prompted
Lele to observe that "there are only limited formal procedures for local
people to influence [party] officials, leaving little more than goodwill to
assure that these officials will, in fact, protect peasant interests."[57] Goodwill proved insufficient to protect peasants against the disruptive effects
of enforced villagization and its aftermath of ecological imbalance and
environmental degradation.

Party representatives soon found themselves competing with administrators and technicians for policy-making supremacy. Disadvantaged
by a lack of technical and administrative expertise, they were compen-
sated by higher salaries and other benefits dispensed as patronage from
party headquarters.[58] Each trying to outdo the other, both sets of elites
emphasized the means of rural development (the hasty proliferation of
villages) over its ultimate ends (self-reliant increases in human welfare
and productivity). To this emphasis, Lele replied, "whether the *ujamaa*
program will be successful in the long run . . . depends on how effectively
the government and the party can generate realistic area-based planning
and ensure grass root support," which in each case required "effective
means of realizing broadly participative economic growth and of improving the welfare of the rural masses."[59] Lele's admonition went basically unheeded until the ecological damage had been done and had
become apparent to party-government leaders as well as to the peasants
compelled to create and live with it.

Since 1981, the national leadership has taken positive steps to re-
build the mutual elite-mass support that once enabled Tanzania to mobi-
lize against colonialism and later to achieve stability on the basis of a
participative and humane governing ideology. New local government
legislation was enacted in 1982, during the same legislative session that
produced a revived cooperative movement. This act reestablished dis-

trict councils and transferred to them the management of all developmental activities. The councils were authorized to levy taxes and to supervise the work of central administrators and technicians now formally employed by a Local Government Service Commission. Future considerations include the councils' direct remuneration of these specialists from local revenues and central government subsidies to enhance the capabilities of councils in poorer districts while not reducing self-help incentives in the rest.[60]

Coupled with a vibrant cooperative movement embracing both export and food crops, the most recent local government initiatives should bring several improvements to rural land use and environmental protection. If taken seriously, district councils will decentralize decision making as well as administration and will thereby lessen the policy distortions emanating from an overloaded national leadership that tends to be physically and conceptually isolated from grass-roots realities. Assisted by skilled personnel, representative councils should also be more disposed toward agricultural development projects reflecting local interests yet protecting the land upon which these interests depend. Finally and perhaps most importantly, a politically strengthened rural sector should eventually be able to place responsible and developmentally constructive demands on the state, its goal setters, and its resources.

In a country committed to a socialist, and therefore a fundamentally statist, and developmental philosophy, semi-independent local institutions may offer the last best chance of reaching an outcome recently proposed by Louis Putterman. "In spite of Tanzania's experience, and even as we look to Tanzania's future, it may be worthwhile to ask whether peasants working to improve their lives by providing themselves with better education and health care, and by raising their productivity, cannot have hope of succeeding notwithstanding the possibly antagonistic aims of governments and peasants' own supposed conservatism."[61] The national responsibility is to help peasants fulfill these goals, at the same time serving that part of the national interest lying outside the peasants' immediate purview. In Tanzania as in Kenya, protecting wildlife and wildlife ecosystems falls within this category.

THE DEVELOPMENTAL ROLE OF WILDLIFE

Solutions to eastern Africa's land use problems and subsistence crises turn not only on the informed cooperation of policy makers and peasant farmers. Wildlife can also play a part in restoring the ecological equilibria that once supported both them and their human competitors. This new role differs from past practice, however. It requires not so much that wild animals be isolated, killed, and sometimes consumed, but rather that they be nurtured in natural habitats available for nonintrusive human enjoyment.

In Kenya, Tanzania, and other African countries, unchecked demographic pressures have created localized environmental stresses that have drastically reduced the survival capacities of people and game animals. One way out of this predicament could be to focus on agricultural land-use reforms while eliminating game animals, whose meat could be used as a temporary food supplement and whose land could be taken over to expand crop and livestock production. Aside from the formidable technical difficulties involved in this approach, and apart form the scientific, political, and moral dilemmas arising from what would amount to a planned extinction of some species, the very real possibility exists that *live* animals could prove far more beneficial to human food and development needs. It is common knowledge that plants are more efficient protein producers than animals. Significant reductions in Africa's chronic food deficits, therefore, depend more on crops than on livestock and other fauna. One large problem is that insufficient foreign exchange is currently on hand to facilitate the development of higher-grade plant strains, to support environmentally safe increases in total crop production, and to help rationalize agricultural services including research and extension, rural credit, transport, storage, processing, and marketing.

Eastern Africa is richly endowed with wildlife and with national park and reserve systems already in place. Here and in Africa's remaining game regions one of the most important potential sources of foreign exchange lies in international tourism. Many tourists will not travel to Africa unless they can experience the full and unique panoply of African game animals in their natural state. If these indigenous spectacles are maintained and made accessible, game animals can serve as indirect but vital instruments of African food sufficiency and rural development. Concomitant improvements in agricultural land use will lessen the deadly ecological chaos that now prevails in the vicinities of most if not all of Africa's wildlife areas. This outcome will serve both people and animals, rendering unnecessary a choice between them, but the plan will work only if tourist and other revenues are specifically dedicated to all sides of the man-land-wildlife triad. In the final analysis, these and all such opportunities are matters of human awareness, will, and public choice. The urgency of the present situation demands that immediate attention be paid to each.

Notes

Notes to the Introduction

1. See Harold T. P. Hayes, *The Last Place on Earth* (New York: Stein and Day, 1977), which offers an informal account of wildlife and land-use issues in contemporary eastern Africa.

2. According to recent United Nations estimates, the total population of Kenya and Tanzania reached 38 million by mid-1982 and will grow to 76 million by the year 2000. The UN also estimates that in 1981 Kenyans and Tanzanians received less than 90 percent of their daily per capita food requirements, and that between 1980 and 1982 per capita food production fell to 88 percent of its 1969–1971 average. World Bank, *World Development Report 1984* (New York: Oxford University Press, 1984), pp. 218, 228, 254, 264.

Notes to Chapter 1

1. Paul Bohannan, *Africa and Africans* (Garden City, NY: The Natural History Press, 1964), p. 197.

2. John Middleton and David Tait (eds.), *Tribes Without Rulers* (London: Routledge and Kegan Paul, 1958), p. 26.

3. Rodger Yeager, *Tanzania: An African Experiment* (Boulder, CO: Westview Press, 1982), pp. 8–24; and Norman N. Miller, *Kenya: The Quest for Prosperity* (Boulder, CO: Westview Press, 1984), pp. 9–33.

4. In this and subsequent discussions, references to Tanzania include only the mainland portion of the country, the former Tanganyika Territory, where the confrontation between humans and indigenous fauna has been the most lasting and recently the most acute.

5. Helge Kjekshus, *Ecology Control and Economic Development in East African History: The Case of Tanganyika, 1850–1950* (Berkeley: University of California Press, 1977), p. 78. It is doubtful whether wildlife would ever have been completely eliminated by farmers and herders. For both humans and their livestock, population growth and density were strictly limited by the weak carrying capacities and endemic diseases of the areas they shared with the indigenous fauna. In any case, some qualification should be made of Kjekshus' generalization about the inherently conflictual nature of human interactions with game animals. In his study of such contacts in southeastern Tanzania, Matzke points out that only some animal species are able and/or predisposed to compete with humans and livestock for the same land and food. See Gordon Matzke, *Wildlife in Tanzanian Settlement Policy: The Case of the Selous* (Syracuse, NY: Maxwell School of Citizenship and Public Affairs, Syracuse University, 1977), p. 2.

6. Kjekshus, *Ecology Control*, p. 50.

7. Ester Boserup, *The Conditions of Agricultural Growth: The Economics of Agrarian Change Under Population Pressure* (Chicago: Aldine Publishing Co., 1965). Kjekshus acknowledges Boserup's contributions to his own thinking about Tanzania.

8. Ibid., p. 41.

9. Ibid., pp. 70, 54. Cf., Judah Matras, *Populations and Societies* (Englewood Cliffs, NJ: Prentice-Hall, Inc., 1973). In tropical Africa, Matras adds, "the amount of land cultivated in any one year is probably about one-thirtieth of the potential cultivable land. Africans do cultivate very intensively when hemmed in topographically, or by enemies, or when otherwise compelled to subsist on much smaller areas than they would like. But the system of shifting cultivation, rather than more intense cultivation, is preferred. So long as abundant land is available, as it is in most of Africa, shifting cultivation yields better returns than settled agriculture in grain per unit of labor" (p. 457).

10. For additional wildlife-related details on this period, see Kjekshus, *Ecology Control*, Chapter 4; and Thomas P. Ofcansky, "A History of Game Preservation in British East Africa, 1895-1963," unpublished Ph.D. dissertation, West Virginia University, 1981, Chapters 3-5.

11. Kjekshus, *Ecology Control*, pp. 177, 184.

12. See Garrett Hardin, "The Tragedy of the Commons," *Science*, 162 (December 13, 1968): 1243–1248. According to Hardin, a tragedy of the commons occurs when people overexploit their common environmental heritage in their immediate self-interests, thereby causing irreversible environmental damage and bringing disaster to them all.

13. World Bank, *Toward Sustained Development in Sub-Saharan Africa: A Joint Program of Action* (Washington: The World Bank, 1984), p. 32.

14. Paul Harrison, *Inside the Third World*, second edition (Harmondsworth, U.K.: Penguin Books, 1981), p. 65.

15. Ibid., p. 69.

Notes to Chapter 2

1. Tanzania, *Third Five Year Plan for Economic and Social Development, 1st July 1976–30th June 1981*, first volume (Dar es Salaam: National Printing Co., n.d.), p. 30.

2. For an analysis of the village settlement program from these perspectives, see Rodger Yeager, "Micropolitical Dimensions of Development and National Integration in Rural Africa: Concepts and an Application," *African Studies Review*, 15 (December 1972): 367–402.

3. This policy shift was legislatively acknowledged in 1975. See Tanzania, *An Act to Provide for the Registration of Villages, the Administration of Registered Villages and the Designation of Ujamaa Villages* (Dar es Salaam: Government Printer, 1975), Part 4, Sec. 16.

4. See Dean E. McHenry, Jr., *Tanzania's Ujamaa Villages: The Implementation of a Rural Development Strategy* (Berkeley: Institute of International Studies, University of California, Berkeley, 1979), Chapter 5; and Adolpho Mascarenhas, "After Villagization—What?" in Bismarck U. Mwansasu and Cranford Pratt (eds.), *Towards Socialism in Tanzania* (Toronto: University of Toronto Press, 1979), pp. 152–156.

5. Rodger Yeager, "Demography and Development Policy in Tanzania," *The Journal of Developing Areas*, 16 (July 1982): 489–509; and Rodger Yeager and Norman N. Miller, *Food Policy in Tanzania: Issues of Production, Distribution, and Sufficiency* (Hanover, NH: Universities Field Staff International, 1982).

6. World Bank, *World Development Report 1984*, p. 228.

7. Boserup, *The Conditions of Agricultural Growth*, p. 94.

8. Tanzania, *Third Five Year Plan for Economic and Social Development*, p. 11.

9. The Hon. Kighoma Malima, quoted in *Africa Now* (December 1982): 57.

10. McHenry, *Tanzania's Ujamaa Villages*, p. 134.

11. Dumont's comments are quoted in the *Sunday News* (Dar es Salaam), July 29, 1979.

12. Michael Chisholm, *Rural Settlement and Land Use: An Essay in Location* (London: Hutchinson University Library, 1962), p. 43.

13. Ibid., p. 71.

14. For a statistical analysis of this decline, see Yeager and Miller, *Food Policy in Tanzania*, p. 7.

15. See Goran Hyden, *Beyond Ujamaa in Tanzania: Underdevelopment and an Uncaptured Peasantry* (Berkeley: University of California Press, 1980).

16. During this period, considerable anxiety was expressed in Tanzanian intellectual circles about the place of tourism in a country committed to achieving socialism, economic self-reliance, and socioeconomic equality. This issue was extensively debated in the local press during 1970, and the various arguments are reproduced in I. G. Shivji (ed.), *Tourism and Socialist Development* (Dar es Salaam: Tanzania Publishing House, 1973).

17. Esrom Maryogo, quoted in Peter Marshall, "Tanzania's Controversial Industry," *Africa Report*, 26 (November-December 1981): 55.

18. For a more detailed account of these events, see Yeager, *Tanzania: An African Experiment*, pp. 99–102.

19. Tanzania, *Third Five Year Plan*, p. 115.

20. These goals were "to generate enough income from the parks and to conserve the environment and to carry out research" and "to promote our parks here in the country and abroad so as to attract more citizens and tourists." Ibid., p. 30.

21. Tanzania, *Third Five Year Development Plan*, second volume, *Investment Analysis* (Dar es Salaam: Government Printer, 1979), p. 17.

22. A. R. E. Sinclair, "Dynamics of the Serengeti Ecosystem: Process and Pattern," in Sinclair and M. Norton-Griffiths (eds.), *Serengeti: The Dynamics of an Ecosystem* (Chicago: University of Chicago Press, 1979), p. 25.

23. United Nations Development Program and UN Food and Agriculture Organization, *East African Livestock Survey: Regional—Kenya, Tanzania, Uganda*, Vol. I, *Development Requirements* (Rome: UNDP and FAO, 1967), p. 151.

24. See T. N. Maletnlema, *Nutrition and Government Policy in the Developing Countries: A Study of the United Republic of Tanzania* (Dar es Salaam: Tanzania Food and Nutrition Centre, 1975), pp. 24 ff.

25. UNDP and FAO, *East African Livestock Survey*, p. 151.

26. See, for example, Peter Mattiessen, *Sand Rivers* (New York: The Viking Press, 1981), which offers a commentary on this situation in the Selous Game Reserve.

27. The psychology of subsistence farming is important in this regard. In one observation,

> some portion of what is grown may be marketed, but it is not enough to make marketing the reason for producing. Given this orientation, farmers may respond to conditions in the marketplace, but will not permit these conditions to color the whole food production process. This situation is quite different from that in which export crops are produced, even when the same people and physical conditions are involved. The reason for growing export crops is to sell them, while the reason for growing food crops is to eat them.

U.S. Department of Agriculture, *Food Problems and Prospects in Sub-Saharan Africa: The Decade of the 1980s* (Washington: Economic Research Service, USDA, August 1981), p. 25.

28. Dharam Ghai et al. (eds.), *Overcoming Rural Underdevelopment: Proceedings of a Workshop on Alternative Agrarian Systems and Rural Development*, held at Arusha, Tanzania, April 4–14, 1979 (Geneva: International Labour Organization, 1979), p. 12.

29. Jean M. Due, "Allocation of Credit to Ujamaa Villages in Tanzania and Small Farms in Zambia," *African Studies Review*, 23 (December 1980): 37; and, Due, *Costs, Returns and Repayment Experience of Ujamaa Villages in Tanzania, 1973-1976* (Washington: University Press of America, 1980), p. 9.

30. Chacha Ndissi, "Ujamaa Villages as a Collective Development Strategy in Tanzania's Economic Development," unpublished Ph.D. dissertation, George Washington University, 1976, pp. 39–70.

31. Michaela von Freyhold, *Ujamaa Villages in Tanzania: Analysis of a Social Experiment* (New York: Monthly Review Press, 1979), p. 105.

32. Helge Kjekshus, "The Tanzanian Villagization Policy: Implementational Lessons and Ecological Dimensions," *Canadian Journal of African Studies*, 11 (1977): 282.

33. On the basis of 1981 food and health estimates, FAO has established an average per capita daily intake of 2,391 calories as the minimum required in Tanzania "to sustain a person at normal levels of activity and health, taking into account age and sex distributions, average body weights and environmental temperatures." The Tanzanian national average in 1981 was 1,985 food calories, representing just 83 percent of minimum requirements. World Bank, *World Development Report 1984*, pp. 264, 283.

34. Average and actual density statistics tell little about the relationship between a population and its agricultural environment and can be quite misleading in this regard. Real densities vary considerably from statistical averages and soils, climate, technology, and other factors decisively influence the number of people a given area can support. Data on average densities are useful in that they provide a semi-empirical base from which to discuss specific settlement patterns and agricultural practices in relation to prevailing environmental conditions. This use is intended for such data in the present study. Cf., Nanda R. Shrestha, "A Preliminary Report on Population Pressure and Land Resources in Nepal," *The Journal of Developing Areas*, 16 (January 1982): 197–212.

35. Ghai, *Overcoming Rural Underdevelopment*, p. 52.

36. Tanzania, *1978 Population Census Preliminary Report* (Dar es Salaam: Bureau of Statistics, Ministry of Finance and Planning, n.d.), p. 172.

37. Tanzania, *An Act to Provide for the Registration of Villages*, Part 2, Sec. 4; and Part 5, Sec. 23, *Directions*.

38. Uma Lele, *The Design of Rural Development: Lessons from Africa* (Baltimore: The Johns Hopkins University Press, 1975), p. 39. As is later pointed out, the Sukuma have now exhausted this land-extensive option.

39. Ghai, *Overcoming Rural Underdevelopment*, p. 88.

40. P. M. van Hekken and H. U. E. Thoden van Velzen, *Land Scarcity and Rural Inequality in Tanzania: Some Case Studies from Rungwe District* (The Hague: Mouton, 1972), pp. 13–14.

41. In its August 27, 1982 edition, for example, the *Wall Street Journal* reported that as a result of villagization, Tanzanian peasants abandoned their outlying fields in favor of those closer to the villages. This partiality caused the nearer plots to lose fertility, which in turn crippled agriculture.

42. C. Gregory Knight, *Ecology and Change: Rural Modernization in an African Community* (New York: Academic Press, 1974), p. xv.

43. The same point was made somewhat differently in a study commissioned by the U.S. Agency for International Development:

> In the decade since Ujamaa villages have been established in Tanzania, there have been situations where the originally designed village plan, geared to a stable population and organized to allow a convenient pattern of homes and agricultural land, has proven unworkable. As new age groups reach the stage where they establish their own farms, new land and buildings are required and a new pattern of housing and land allocation is needed. As the number of people in the village grows larger, it is more and more difficult to keep the centralized village plan because of the increasing distance to walk to the fields.

B. L. Turner et al., *Trends and Interrelationships in Food, Population, and Energy in Eastern Africa: A Preliminary Analysis*, Vol. 1, *Overview* (Worcester, MA: Program for International Development, Clark University, December 1980), p. 41.

44. S. Nieuwolt, "The Influence of Rainfall on Rural Population Distribution in Tanzania," *The Journal of Tropical Geography*, 44 (June 1977): 43–56. According to this analysis, overpopulated districts included Magu, Bariadi, Maswa, Kilosa, and Morogoro Rural. Pockets of overpopulation were discovered in Mbulu, Hanang, Arumeru, Rombo, Moshi Rural, Hai, and Lushoto. Only Iringa Rural was found to be underpopulated for its rainfall potential.

45. J. P. Moffett (ed.), *Handbook of Tanganyika*, second edition (Dar es Salaam: Government Printer, 1958), p. 453.

46. Charles Elliott, *Rural Poverty in Africa*, Occasional Paper No. 12, Centre for Development Studies, University College of Swansea (Norwich, U.K.: Geo Abstracts Ltd., 1980), p. 27.

47. Shrestha, "A Preliminary Report," p. 206.

48. See James E. Kocher, *Rural Development and Fertility Change in Tropical Africa: Evidence from Tanzania* (East Lansing: African Rural Economy Program, Michigan State University, 1979). Conducted in the early 1970s, Kocher's study focused on the relationship of economic development to fertility and population growth in present-day Hai District and in southern Lushoto District.

49. Chisholm, *Rural Settlement and Land Use*, p. 49.

50. Hans Ruthenberg, "Some Characteristics of Smallholder Farming in

Tanzania," in Ruthenberg (ed.), *Smallholder Farming and Smallholder Development in Tanzania* (Munich: Weltforum Verlag, 1968), pp. 327–328.

51. Ibid., pp. 334–335.

52. In Boserup's interpretation,

> when the stage is reached where all able-bodied members of the rural communities, males and females, young and old, are labouring from sunrise to sunset all year, the community has reached the point where additional investment can be undertaken only if current work is reduced and per capita food consumption declines. The introduction of agricultural communes in China was no doubt an attempt to avoid a decline of per capita food production by pushing the performance of work to this point of maximum employment.

Boserup, *The Conditions of Agricultural Growth*, p. 104.

53. Mette Monsted and Parveen Walji, *A Demographic Analysis of East Africa: A Sociological Interpretation* (New York: Africana Publishing Co., 1978), p. 139.

54. Manfred Attems, "Permanent Cropping in the Usambara Mountains: The Relevancy of the Minimum Benefit Thesis," in Ruthenberg, *Smallholder Farming*, pp. 141–167. Cf., Kocher, *Rural Development*, pp. 27–39.

55. Attems, "Permanent Cropping," p. 162.

56. Paul Stephen Maro, "Population and Land Resources in Northern Tanzania: The Dynamics of Change, 1920–1970," unpublished Ph.D. dissertation, The University of Minnesota, 1974.

57. Ibid., p. 277.

58. In early 1983, Tanzanian factories were reportedly running at about 30 percent of capacity. This production level may have declined even further in more recent years.

59. Dietrich von Rhotenhan, "Cotton Farming in Sukumaland: Cash Cropping and its Implications," in Ruthenberg, *Smallholder Farming*, pp. 53, 76.

60. Ibid., p. 77.

61. Ibid., pp. 85–86.

62. W. Mackenzie, "Conflicts and Obstacles in Livestock Development in Tanzania," *East African Journal of Rural Development*, 5 (1972): 82.

63. Ibid., p. 83.

64. UNDP and FAO, *East African Livestock Survey*, Vol. II, *Development Plans*, p. 64.

65. A. M. O'Conner, *An Economic Geography of East Africa* (New York: Frederick A. Praeger Publishers, 1966), pp. 236–237. Cf., UNDP and FAO, *East African Livestock Survey*, Vol. I, p. 89, and Vol. II, p. 51; and R. K. Davis, "The Trade-Off Between Wildlife and Livestock in One Ranching Area in Kenya," *East African Journal of Rural Development*, 5 (1972): 73–80.

66. J. J. R. Grimsdell, "Changes in Populations of Resident Ungulates," in Sinclair and Norton-Griffiths, *Serengeti*, p. 359.

67. S. J. McNaughton, "Grassland-Herbivore Dynamics," in ibid., p. 73.

68. Ghai, *Overcoming Rural Underdevelopment*, p. 92.

69. This outpouring from the north has already commenced, following the party-government's encouragement of landless farmers in Kilimanjaro Region to form villages in lightly populated, albeit less arable, portions of Morogoro Region.

70. See Eckhard Baum, "Land Use in the Kilombero Valley: From Shifting Cultivation Towards Permanent Farming," in Ruthenberg, *Smallholder Farming*, pp. 24–35.

71. Ibid., pp. 26–27, 35–39.

72. Ibid., p. 47.

73. Ralph Jätzold and Eckhard Baum, *The Kilombero Valley: Characteristic Features of the Economic Geography of a Semihumid East African Flood Plain and its Margins* (Munich: Weltforum Verlag, 1968), p. 41.

74. Cf., for example, Ndissi, "Ujamaa Villages," a study of two village communities in Iringa Rural District, to the east of the Ruaha National Park.

75. Kjekshus, *Ecology Control*, pp. 177–178.

76. Matzke, *Wildlife in Tanzanian Settlement Policy*, pp. 18–43. See also Matzke, "Large Animals, Small Settlements, and Big Problems: A Study of Overlapping Space Preferences in Southern Tanzania," unpublished Ph.D. dissertation, Syracuse University, 1975, pp. 181–184.

77. Matzke, *Wildlife in Tanzanian Settlement Policy*, p. 97.

78. Matzke, "Large Animals," p. 184.

79. Matzke, *Wildlife in Tanzanian Settlement Policy*, p. 110.

80. Brian Nicholson, quoted in Matthiessen, *Sand Rivers*, p. 183.

81. Quoted in *Maryknoll* (April 1983): 60–61.

Notes to Chapter 3

1. Portions of this chapter were originally published as *Wildlife-Wild Death: Kenya's Man-Animal Equation* (Hanover, NH: Universities Field Staff International, 1982). I am grateful to Rodger Yeager for editing the present version and for supplementing it with additional demographic, economic, and political analyses.

2. The implications of these and other long-term demographic trends are further explored in chapter 4.

3. World Bank *Towards Sustained Development in Sub-Saharan Africa*, p. 77.

4. Personal communication, Nairobi, June 1981.

5. Karen A. Carlson, "The Kenya Wildlife Conservation Campaign: A Description and Critical Study of Intercultural Persuasion," unpublished Ph.D. dissertation, Northwestern University, 1969.

6. Bernhard and Michael Grzimek, *Serengeti Darf Nicht Sterben* (Berlin: Verlag Ullstein, 1959).

7. Kenya, *Economic Survey 1983* (Nairobi: Central Bureau of Statistics, Ministry of Economic Planning and Development, 1983), pp. 113, 114, 116. Similar biases in agricultural extension are discussed in chapter 4.

8. Ibid., pp. 33, 119. A cooperative Smallholder Production Services Credit Programme was begun in 1975, with the following purposes:

> . . . to develop the capacity within the co-operative system, to organize and implement a programme which will provide comprehensive production and marketing services for food crop production to smallholders who have potential for increasing their production but have not previously benefited substantially from such services . . . and to build the existing co-operative network into a fully integrated supply, marketing and credit system capable of supporting the typical subsistence-oriented producer so that he can improve his economic status and contribute to the food supply of the country. (Ibid., p. 41)

After dispensing slightly more than $3 million, the program was abruptly terminated in 1982.

9. See chapter 4, footnote 50.

10. For example, Donald L. Capone, "Wildlife, Man and Competition for Land in Kenya: A Geographical Analysis," unpublished Ph.D. dissertation, Michigan State University, 1972.

11. Wildlife disease research is better integrated. For a partly annotated bibliography of studies in this area, see Lars Karstad, *Infections, Parasites, and Diseases of African Wild Animals* (Ottawa: International Development Research Centre, 1978). See also United Nations Food and Agriculture Organization and UN Development Program, *Wildlife Disease Research: Kenya. Project Findings and Recommendations* (Rome: FAO, 1978).

12. *Sunday Times* (London), August 12, 19, 26, 1975.

13. Personal communication, Nairobi, June 1981.

14. Ian Parker, ibid.

15. Harold D. Nelson (ed.), *Kenya: A Country Study*, third edition (Washington: U.S. Department of the Army, 1983), p. 76.

16. The World Bank has estimated that, as early as 1972, Nyanza, Western, and Eastern provinces were burdened with population surpluses of 840,000, 100,000, and 300,000 people, respectively. Central Province experienced no surplus population but likewise no excess land capacity at this time. Rift Valley and Coast provinces enjoyed surplus capacities of 370,000 and 1,250,000 people, probably resulting from the large number of marginal but still arable localities in these jurisdictions. No data were available for North-Eastern Province. Rashid Faruqee et al., *Kenya: Population and Development* (Washington: Development Economics Department, East Africa Country Programs Department, The World Bank, 1980), p. 45.

17. Miller, *Kenya: The Quest for Prosperity*, p. 86.

18. Capone, "Wildlife, Man and Competition," pp. 91–92.

19. Ibid., p. 93. By 1985, the average population density of Kajiado District

has risen to about ten people per square kilometer. In this and the following cases, district-level density estimates are obtained and extrapolated from Kenya, *Kenya Population Census 1979*, Vol. 1 (Nairobi: Central Bureau of Statistics, Ministry of Economic Planning and Development, June 1981), Table 1, "Population by Sex and Sub-Location," pp. 45–103.

20. Capone, "Wildlife, Man and Competition," pp. 104–105.

21. Ibid., p. 106.

22. Ibid., p. 178. For the details of this case, see Chapter 4 of Capone's manuscript, "The Human Invasion and the Displacement of Wildlife: Pioneer Settlement on the Arid Fringes." Displacement does not only occur as a consequence of smallholder migration into wildlife areas. It can also result from an expansion of land-extensive cash-cropping, as demonstrated in Narok District of Rift Valley Province where large-scale wheat production has greatly diminished the seasonal rangeland available to migratory game animals protected by the Maasai Mara National Reserve.

23. In 1983, agricultural activities accounted for more than 35 percent of the Kenyan gross domestic product, and this percentage included only that part of the agricultural product officially marketed and thusly counted. Kenya, *Economic Survey 1984* (Nairobi: Central Bureau of Statistics, Ministry of Finance and Planning, 1984), p. 17.

24. U.S. Congress, Office of Technology Assessment, "Solving Africa's Food Problems Requires Long-Term Commitment," press release, Washington, January 31, 1985. For further analysis of OTA's position on this subject, see *Africa Tomorrow: Issues in Technology, Agriculture, and U.S. Foreign Aid* (Washington: U.S. Government Printing Office, 1985).

25. In late 1984 and early 1985, these other food-deficit countries consisted of Angola, Botswana, Burundi, Burkina Faso (Upper Volta), Lesotho, Niger, Rwanda, Senegal, Somalia, Sudan, Zambia, and Zimbabwe.

26. Faruqee, *Kenya: Population and Development*, p. 52. See also Kenya, *Child Nutrition in Rural Kenya* (Nairobi: Central Bureau of Statistics, Ministry of Economic Planning and Community Affairs, n.d.).

27. Faruqee, *Kenya: Population and Development*, pp. 55–58. See also J. Heyer and J. K. Waweru, "The Development of Small Farm Areas," in J. Heyer et al. (eds.), *Agricultural Development in Kenya: An Economic Assessment* (Nairobi: Oxford University Press, 1976).

28. Faruqee, *Kenya: Population and Development*, p. 58; and R. von Kaufmann, "The Development of Range Land Areas," in Heyer, *Agricultural Development in Kenya*, p. 225.

29. See Nelson, *Kenya: A Country Study*, pp. 141–155; and Capone, "Wildlife, Man and Competition," pp. 53–58.

30. The World Bank recognized possibilities of these types some years ago in its *Argicultural Sector Survey Report for Kenya* (Washington: The World Bank, 1973).

31. This inventory is suggested by the field work of Joseph Popp, an American ecologist who has studied Maasai Mara.

32. Kenya, *Statement on the Future of Wildlife Management Policy in Kenya*, Sessional Paper No. 3 of 1975 (Nairobi: Government Printer, 1975), p. 8.

33. Personal communication, Nairobi, May 1981.

34. Lele, *The Design of Rural Development*, p. 150.

35. *The Washington Post National Weekly Edition*, September 10, 1984.

36. Kenya, *Economic Survey 1984*, p. 177. This change occurred between 1982 and 1983 and was most directly brought about by the coup attempt of August 1982. On the other hand, deteriorating economic conditions in the rural and urban areas are held largely responsible for the strikes and civil protests of 1981, which provided justifications if not incentives for the attempted military takeover.

37. For a general discussion of the developmental advantages of nongovernmental actors and organizations, see Goran Hyden, *No Shortcuts to Progress: African Development Management in Perspective* (Berkeley: University of California Press, 1983), Chapter 5.

Notes to Chapter 4

1. Quoted in *Science News*, 124 (November 5, 1983): 301. For a summary of research on elephant heart disease possibly influenced by the same environmental factors, see Norman Myers, *A Wealth of Wild Species: Storehouse for Human Welfare* (Boulder, CO: Westview Press, 1983), p. 120.

2. Hugh Winsor, "East African Adventures," *World Press Review* (December 1983): 62.

3. By 1982, Kenya's total fertility rate had climbed to 8.0, the highest in the world. Total fertility is an estimate of the number of children that would be born to a woman if she were to reproduce, throughout her reproductive cycle, at her country's average fertility rates from puberty to menopause. World Bank, *World Development Report 1984*, p. 256.

4. Ibid., p. 254. The World Band estimates that Kenya will attain a net reproduction rate of 1 by the year 2030. The net reproduction rate is a projection of the total number of daughters that will be born to a newborn girl, considering her society's average fertility rates and mortality rate. A net reproduction rate of 1 means that the birth rate is constant and equal to the death rate and the population's age structure is also constant. However, "a population tends to grow even after fertility has declined to replacement level because past high growth rates will have produced an age distribution with a relatively high proportion of women in, or still to enter, the reproductive ages" (Ibid., p. 281).

5. Ibid., pp. 94, 228, 248, 264; and World Bank, *World Development Report 1978* (Washington: The World Bank, August 1978), p. 96.

6. David K. Leonard, *Reaching the Peasant Farmer: Organization Theory and Practice in Kenya* (Chicago: University of Chicago Press, 1977), pp. 193, 194.

7. John W. Harbeson, *Nation-Building in Kenya: The Role of Land Reform* (Evanston, IL: Northwestern University Press, 1973), p. 347. See also Henry Bienen, *Kenya: The Politics of Participation and Control* (Princeton, NJ: Princton University Press, 1974), pp. 161–182.

8. *Kenya Standard* (Nairobi), February 12, 1981.

9. See Allan Frank, "The Market's Discipline," *Forbes* (November 22, 1982): 102–106.

10. Leonard Berry, *Eastern Africa Country Profiles: Kenya* (Worcester, MA: Program for International Development, Clark University, 1980), p. 54.

11. In 1982, Kenya controlled about $248 million in international currency reserves, enough for less than six weeks of import coverage. The country's balance-of-payments deficit had growth from $49 million in 1970 to $509 million by 1982. World Bank, *World Development Report 1984*, p. 244.

12. Kenya, *National Food Policy*, Sessional Paper No. 4 of 1981 (Nairobi: Government Printer, 1981), p. 8.

13. World Bank, *World Development Report 1984*, p. 164. FAO assesses population-supporting land capabilities on the basis of soils, climate, and available agricultural technologies.

14. Ibid., p. 165. These other countries include Botswana, Burundi, Ethiopia, Lesotho, Malawi, Mauritania, Namibia, Niger, Nigeria, Rwanda, Senegal, Somalia, and Uganda. They account for one-third of tropical Africa's total land area and for about one-half of its 1981 population.

15. Ibid. The other African countries sharing this predicament are Burundi, Lesotho, Mauritania, Niger, Rwanda, and Somalia.

16. In all likelihood, population control programs will play little role in overcoming Kenya's food problem. Public expenditures on population activities totaled less than $12 million in 1980, or about 71 cents per capita. Although specifically committed to family planning in addition to maternal and child health, the official population policy is characterized as "weak" by the UN Fund for Population Activities. Ibid., pp. 149, 200.

17. Ibid., pp. 254, 260.

18. Ibid., p. 248.

19. Ibid., p. 94.

20. Yeager and Miller, *Food Policy in Tanzania*, passim; and Norman N. Miller, *East Africa's New Decade of Doubt. Part I: Kenya and Tanzania* (Hanover, NH: American Universities Field Staff, 1980). For a neo-Marxist critique of Tanzanian rural credit policy, see James H. Mittelman, *Underdevelopment and the Transition to Socialism: Mozambique and Tanzania* (New York: Academic Press, 1981), pp. 190–205.

21. Like Kenya, Tanzania will have to rely on such improvements to balance population with food availability. Tanzania spends only about 18 cents per capita on population programs, and these are devoted almost entirely to maternal and child health. World Bank, *World Development Report 1984*, pp. 149, 200. For further analysis of this policy choice, see Yeager, "Demography and Development Policy"; Kocher, *Rural Development*; and UN Fund for Population

Activities, *Tanzania: Report of Mission on Needs Assessment for Population Assistance* (New York: UNFPA, 1979).

22. Zaki Ergas, "Why Did the Ujamaa Policy Fail?—Towards a Global Analysis," *The Journal of Modern African Studies*, 18 (September 1980): 387–410. Also see Joel Samoff, "Crises and Socialism in Tanzania," *The Journal of Modern African Studies*, 19 (June 1981): 279–306.

23. For an unofficial translation of the party guidelines as they apply to agriculture, see *Daily News* (Dar es Salaam), October 13, 1982. President Nyerere's speech to the 1982 party conference appears in ibid., October 22 and 23, 1982. In his words, "the truth is that these few villages with a large ujamaa shamba [communal farm] are the ones which lead in development as a whole, as well as in the progress of agriculture." The accumulated evidence suggests that this statement is more accurate for export crop villages than for food crop communities and applies best to showcase villages singled out for heavy inputs of agricultural credit and technical assistance.

24. "It must be stated categorically that the economic policy of Chama Cha Mapinduzi aims at satisfying the basic requirements of every person in food as well as to give our nation the capacity and ability to be self-reliant in her development needs and requirements now and in the future." Ibid., October 13, 1982.

25. Ibid., October 13 and 20, 1982.

26. For an examination of this problem by one of Tanzania's leading economic analysts, see M. E. Mlambiti, "Problems of Food Production in Tanzania: Who is to Blame?" paper presented at the Annual Conference of the Agricultural Economics Society of Tanzania, Morogoro, December 1981.

27. *Daily News*, October 22, 1982.

28. Ibid., October 23, 1982.

29. Ibid.

30. Ibid., emphasis added.

31. *President Nyerere's Address at the Inauguration of Sokoine University of Agriculture Morogoro: 26th September 1984* (mimeo.), p. 2.

32. More than a decade ago, Popovic suggested one possible funding strategy. "Investments in the North Tanzanian game sanctuaries will soonest become profitable and deserve priority. From a conservation point of view, however, it would also be desirable to give the game reserves in other areas full protection and as far as financial means become available to designate further areas as national parks." Vojislav Popovic, *Tourism in Eastern Africa* (Munich: Weltforum Verlag, 1972), p. 151.

33. For an interesting case study in this regard, see Alan H. Jacobs, "Pastoral Development in Tanzanian Maasailand," paper presented at the 1980 Annual Meeting of the African Studies Association of the United States, Philadelphia, October 1980. In this paper, Jacobs explores the failure of a United States-sponsored Maasai Range Development Program. For additional commentary on this project by its former field director, see Jon Moris, *Managing Induced Rural Development* (Bloomington: International Development Institute, Indiana University, 1981), pp. 99–113. International assistance activities are further discussed

in this chapter from the standpoint of their broader impact on domestic political leadership in Kenya and Tanzania.

34. Between 1978 and 1981, for example, the following United States doctoral dissertations focused on northern Tanzania alone: Mary T. Howard, "Kwashiokor on Kilimanjaro: The Social Handling of Malnutrition," Michigan State University (1980); Chrysanth L. Kamuzora, "The Dynamics of Labor in African Smallholder Agriculture: The Sources of Labor for a New Cash Crop, Tea, in Bukoba District, Tanzania," University of Pennsylvania (1978); Michael K. McCall, "The Diffusion of Regional Underdevelopment: Articulation of Capital and Peasantry in Sukumaland, Tanzania," Northwestern University (1980); James T. O'Rourke, "Grazing Rate and System Trial over Five Years in a Medium-Height Grassland of Northern Tanzania," The University of Arizona (1978); and Gerritt van der Wees, "Mobility and Choice of Technology in the Development Process in Rural Areas of Developing Countries: A Study of Change in Northwest Tanzania," The University of Washington (1981). For examples of recently published research, see the References.

35. Carl K. Eicher, "Facing Up to Africa's Food Crisis," *Foreign Affairs*, 61 (Fall 1982): 168-169.

36. M. Norton-Griffiths, "The Influence of Grazing, Browsing, and Fire on the Vegetation Dynamics of the Serengeti," in Sinclair and Norton-Griffiths, *Serengeti*, p. 347.

37. Davis, "The Trade-Off Between Wildlife and Livestock," p. 79.

38. Matzke, *Wildlife in Tanzanian Settlement Policy*, pp. 3-5, 60 ff. Matzke determined that some of Selous' grassland species (elephant, warthog, waterbuck, impala, wildebeest, and zebra) show a strong preference for areas humans had once settled and that certain woodland ungulates (hartebeest and duiker) display no special liking for these habitats.

39. Ibid., p. 111.

40. Tanzanian Food and Nutrition Centre, *Data Report on the Food and Nutrition Situation in Tanzania, 1972/73-1976/77* (Dar es Salaam: Department of Planning, TFNC, March 1978).

41. Tanzania, *Bulletin of Food Crop Production Statistics, 1963/64-1977/78* (Dar es Salaam: Statistics Section, Planning Division, Ministry of Agriculture, April 1979), p. i.

42. Eicher, "Facing Up to Africa's Food Crisis," p. 168.

43. For a brief description of this research, see Thomas Land, "Environment Management in Nigeria," *Worldview*, 25 (October 1982): 16-17.

44. Maro, "Population and Land Resources," pp. 276-277.

45. Ndissi, "Ujamaa Villages," pp. 116-117.

46. Cf., Leonard, *Reaching the Peasant Farmer*, passim.

47. Quoted in *A Shift in the Wind 16: Africa* (San Francisco: The Hunger Project, August 1983), p. 4.

48. "US Response to Africa's Food Needs" (Washington: Bureau of Public Affairs, U.S. Department of State, August 1984); and *Africa: The Potential for*

Higher Food Production, Special Report No. 125 (Washington: Bureau of Public Affairs, U.S. Department of State, April 1985), p. 8.

49. Concerning the organizationally disruptive effects of nonmilitary aid, see Elliott R. Morss, "Institutional Destruction Resulting from Donor and Project Proliferation in Sub-Saharan African Countries," *World Development*, 12 (1984): 465–470.

50. Kenya offers a tentative example of this cooperation in the 1977 World Bank loan (discussed in chapter 3) for wildlife protection and national park development. The loan provided for the establishment of a wildlife planning unit in the central government. This organization is intended to carry out ecological studies of Kenya's national parks and reserves and to develop plans for the future utilization of these areas. Bilateral Canadian aid has continued to fund the unit, but by 1985 its work was still mostly confined to agenda setting.

51. "Feeding a Hungry World," *Resources*, 76 (Spring 1984): 7.

52. Hyden, *No Shortcuts to Progress*, p. 7.

53. Bienen, *Kenya*, pp. 183–184.

54. Hyden, *No Shortcuts to Progress*, p. 19.

55. Ibid., p. 52.

56. William W. Murdoch, *The Poverty of Nations: The Political Economy of Hunger and Population* (Baltimore: The Johns Hopkins University Press, 1980), p. 304.

57. Lele, *The Design of Rural Development*, p. 153.

58. See Louis A. Picard, "Attitudes and Development: The District Administration in Tanzania," *African Studies Review*, 23 (December 1980): 60. For a commentary on the growing tendency of the *Chama Cha Mapinduzi* party organization to be used as a vehicle for patronage, see Hyden, *No Shortcuts to Progress*, p. 43.

59. Lele, *The Design of Rural Development*, p. 161.

60. See B. M. Nyiti, *Popular Participation in Rural Development: Tanzania Experience* (Dar es Salaam: Prime Minister's Office, Government of Tanzania, October 1983), pp. 16–19. For a recent statement of the agricultural strategy that should benefit from these political reforms, see Tanzania, Ministry of Agriculture, *The Agricultural Policy of Tanzania* (Dar es Salaam: Government Printer, March 1983).

61. Louis Putterman, "Tanzanian and African Socialism: Comment on Weaver and Kronemer," *World Development*, 12 (1984): 463.

References

Wildlife

Asibey, E. "Wildlife as a Source of Protein in Africa South of the Sahara." *Biological Conservation*, 6 (1974): 32–39.

Blancou, L. "Destruction and Protection of the Fauna of French Equatorial Africa and of French West Africa, Part II, The Larger Mammals." *African Wildlife*, 14 (1960): 10–108.

Bolton, M. "Last Chance for Swayne's Hartebeest." *Biological Conservation*, 3 (1971): 147–148.

_____ . *Ethiopian Wildlands*. London: Collins and Havrill Press, 1976.

Butynski, T. M. and W. von Richter. "Wildlife Management in Botswana." *Wildlife Society Bulletin*, 3 (1975): 19–24.

Campbell, H. C. "The National Park and Reserve System in Botswana." *Biological Conservation*, 5 (1973): 7–14.

Casebeer, R. L. "Coordinating Range and Wildlife Management in Kenya." *Journal of Forestry*, 76 (1978): 374–375.

Chapuis, M. "Evolution and Protection of the Wildlife of Morocco." *African Wildlife*, 15 (1961): 107–112.

Child, G "Wildlife Utilization and Management in Botswana." *Biological Conservation*, 3 (1970): 18–22.

Cousins, D. "Man's Exploitation of the Gorilla." *Biological Conservation*, 13 (1978): 287–297.

162

Curry-Lindahl, K. *Let Them Live: A World Survey of Animals Threatened With Extinction.* New York: William Morrow and Co., 1972.

_____ . "War and White Rhino." *Oryx,* 11 (1972): 263–267.

_____ . "Man in Madagascar." *Defenders of Wildlife,* 50 (1975): 164–169.

Eckholm, E. "Disappearing Species: The Social Challenge." *Worldwatch Paper* 22. Washington: Worldwatch Institute, July 1978.

Ehrlich, P. and A. Ehrlich. *Extinction: The Causes and Consequences of the Disappearance of Species.* New York: Oxford University Press, 1981.

Field, C. R. and I. C. Ross. "The Savanna Ecology of Kidepo Valley National Park." *East African Wildlife Journal,* 14 (1976): 1–15.

Groom, A. F. G. "Squeezing Out the Mountain Gorilla." *Oryx,* 12 (1973): 207–215.

Guggisberg, C. A. W. *S.O.S. Rhino: A Survival Book.* London: Andre Deutsch, 1966.

Guillarmod, A. J. "Point of No Return?" *African Wildlife,* 29 (1975): 28–31.

Hamilton, P. H. and J. M. King. "The Fate of Black Rhinoceroses Released in Nairobi National Park." *East African Wildlife Journal,* 7 (1969): 73–83.

Harcourt, A. H. "Virunga Gorillas—The Case Against Translocations." *Oryx,* 13 (1977): 469–472.

Harcourt, A. H. and K. Curry-Lindahl. "Conservation of the Mountain Gorilla and its Habitat in Rwanda." *Environmental Conservation,* 6 (1979): 143–147.

Hardin, G. "Of Profits and Protoplasm: Destroying Wildlife in the People's Name." *Defenders of Wildlife,* 56 (1981): 22–25.

Hillman, K. "Trying to Save the Rhino." *Swara,* 2 (1979): 22–27.

Homewood, K. M. "Can the Tana Mangabey Survive?" *Oryx,* 13 (1975): 53–59.

Hutagalung, T. and J. Sawe. *Progress Report on the Implementation of Recommendations on Regional Programmes in the Conservation and Management of African Wildlife.* Geneva: United Nations Joint Inspection Unit, February 1983.

Huxley, J. *The Conservation of Wildlife and Natural Habitats in Central and East Africa.* Paris: UNESCO, 1960.

Jackson, P. "The Future of Elephants and Rhinos in Africa." *Ambio,* 7 (1982): 202–206.

Jahnke, H. *Conservation and Utilization of Wildlife in Uganda: A Study in Environmental Economics.* Munich: IFO—Institut für Wirtschaftsforschung, 1975.

Jeffery, S. M. "A Preliminary Report on Trading in Bushmeat, Ivory, Skins, and Live Animals in Liberia." *Journal of the Ghana Wildlife Society,* 1 (1976): 23–25.

Lever, C. "Wildlife Conservation in the Southern Sudan." *Oryx,* 17 (1983): 190–193.

Lewin, R. "Parks: How Big is Big Enough?" *Science,* 225 (August 10, 1984): 611–612.

Lewis, J. G. and R. T. Wilson. "The Plight of Swayne's Hartebeest in Ethiopia." *Oryx*, 13 (1977): 490–494.

Makacha, S. et al. "The Conservation of the Black Rhinoceros in the Ngorongoro Crater, Tanzania." *African Journal*, 17 (1979): 97–103.

Marsh, C. "Monkeys and Conservation on the Lower Tana River." *African Wildlife Foundation News*, 10 (1975): 11–13.

Martin, E. B. *The International Trade in Rhinoceros Products.* Gland, Switzerland: International Union for Conservation of Nature and Natural Resources/World Wildlife Fund, 1980.

_____ . "The Decline in the Trade of Rhinoceros Horn." *Swara*, 6 (1983): 10–15.

Martin, E. B. and I.S.C. Parker. "Trade in African Rhino Horn." *Oryx*, 15 (1979): 153–158.

_____ . "Exploding Some Myths About Rhino Horns." *Africana*, 7 (1980): 12–13.

Mbuvi, D. M. *Wildlife Education and Extension Services in Kenya.* Nairobi: Ministry of Environmental and Natural Resources, Government of Kenya, 1980.

Myers, N. "A Scourge Upon the Land." *International Wildlife*, 9 (1979): 34–35.

_____ . *The Sinking Ark.* London: Pergamon Press, 1979.

_____ . "The Problem of Disappearing Species: What Can We Do?" *Ambio*, 5 (1980): 229–234.

Nchunga, M. L. *The Potential for Commercial Use of Wildlife in Some Northeastern Tuli Block Farms.* College Station: Texas A&M University Press, 1978.

Nimir, M. B. and S. A. R. Hakim. "Wildlife Conservation in the Arid Zone of the Sudan." In J. A. Mabbutt (ed.), *Proceedings of the Khartoum Workshop on Arid Lands Management: The University of Khartoum and the United Nations University, October 22–26, 1978.* Tokyo: United Nations University, 1979, pp. 40–44.

Ole-Saibull, S. A. "The Policy Process: The Case of Conservation in the Ngorongoro Highlands." *Tanzania Notes and Records*, 83 (1978): 101–115.

Petrides, G. A. *Advisory Report on Wildlife and National Parks in Nigeria.* New York: American Commission for International Wildlife Protection, 1965.

Price, S. " Didn't Know My Country Was So Beautiful." *International Wildlife*, 9 (1979): 4–11.

Riney, T. *Conservation and Management of African Wildlife.* Rome: United Nations Food and Agriculture Organization, 1967.

Robinson, P. T. "WIldlife Trends in Liberia and Sierra Leone." *Oryx*, 12 (1971): 117–122.

Rodgers, W. A. and J. D. Lobo. "Elephant Control and Legal Ivory Exploitation: 1920–1976." *Tanzania Notes and Records*, 84, 85 (1980): 25–54.

Rogalsky, D. R. "Wildlife Paying Its Own Way: Tourism as a Justification for

Wildlife Conservation." Nairobi: Sixth African Wildlife Conference, *Proceedings*, 1980.

Sawe, J. A. *Report on Regional Training Programmes in African Wildlife Management at Mweka and Garoua*. Rome: United Nations Food and Agriculture Organization, 1979.

Schaller, G. *The Year of the Gorilla*. Chicago: University of Chicago Press, 1964.

Sheldrick, D. *The Orphans of Tsavo*. London: Collins and Havrill Press, 1966.

Simonetta, A. M. "The Significance of the Uniqueness of Somali Wildlife." *Somali Range Bulletin*, 11 (1981): 8–12.

Soule, B. A. et al. "Benign Neglect: A Model of Faunal Collapse in the Game Reserves of East Africa." *Biological Conservation*, 15 (1979): 258–267.

Spinage, C. A. et al. "Food Selection by the Grant's Gazelle." *African Journal of Ecology*, 18 (1980): 19–25.

Struhsaker, T. T. "Rain Forest Conservation in African Primates," *Primates*, 13 (1972): 103–109.

Taiti, S. "Ecological Criteria of Land Evaluation for Wildlife." *Kenya Soil Survey*, 11 (1977): 61–72.

Thorsell, J. W. *National Parks, Reserves and Protected Areas of Kenya*. Nairobi: Ministry of Environmental and Natural Resources, Government of Kenya, November 1980.

Tomlinson, D. N. S. "Nature Conservation in Rhodesia: A Review." *Biological Conservation*, 15 (1980): 159–177.

Vaclay, E. and J. Vaguer. "Conservation of East African Nature." *Silvaecultura Tropica et Subtropica*, 4 (1976): 139–169.

Western, D. *A Wildlife Guide and a Natural History of Amboseli*. Nairobi: General Printers, Ltd., 1983.

Land Use

Acock, A. M. "Land Policies and Economic Development in East and Central Africa." *Agricultural Economics Bulletin for Africa*, 9 (1962): 1–54.

Almy, S. W. "The Response of Agricultural Systems to Natural Increase: The History of a High-Potential Region in Kenya." *Studies in Third World Societies*, 8 (1979): 57–95.

Berry, E. and L. Berry. *Land Use in Tanzania by Districts*. Dar es Salaam: Bureau of Resource Assessment and Land Use Planning, University of Dar es Salaam, 1969.

Berry, L. et al. *Human Adjustment to Agricultural Drought in Tanzania: Pilot Investigations*. Dar es Salaam: Bureau of Resource Assessment and Land Use Planning, University of Dar es Salaam, 1971.

Bunderson, W. T. "Ecological Separation of Wild and Domestic Mammals in an

East African Ecosystem." Unpublished Ph.D. dissertation, Utah State University, 1981.

Burley, J. *Obstacles to Tree Planting in Arid and Semi-Arid Lands: Comparative Case Studies from India and Kenya.* Tokyo: United Nations University, 1982.

Chambers, R. *Managing Rural Development.* Uppsala, Sweden: Scandinavian Institute of African Studies, 1974.

Clayton, E. S. "Kenya Agriculture and I.L.O. Employment Mission—Six Years Later." *Journal of Modern African Studies,* 16 (1978): 311-318.

Clough, R. H. *Some Economic Aspects of Land Settlement in Kenya: A Report on an Economic Survey in Four Districts in Western Kenya, 1963-1964.* Njoro, Kenya: Egerton College, January 1965.

Danfors, E. et al. *Land Use in Kenya and Tanzania.* Stockholm: Royal College of Forestry, 1975.

Darkob, M. B. K. "Population Expansion and Desertification in Tanzania." *Deserification Control,* 2 (1982): 26-33.

Deme, L. W. "The Agricultural Tax in Socialist Ethiopia: A Preliminary Evaluation of the Tax System." *Ethiopian Journal of Development Research,* 3 (1979): 1-14.

El-Arifi, M. "Some Aspects of Local Government and Environmental Management in the Sudan." In J. A. Mabbutt (ed.), *Proceedings of the Khartoum Workshop on Arid Lands Management: The University of Khartoum and the United Nations University, October 22-26, 1978.* Tokyo: United Nations University, 1979, pp. 36-39.

Emmanuel, H. W. *Land Tenure, Land-Use and Development in the Awash Valley, Ethiopia.* Madison: Land Tenure Center, University of Wisconsin, 1975.

Ford, J. *The Role of Trypanosomiasis in the African Ecology.* London: Clarendon Press, 1971.

Fumagalli, C. T. "Evaluation of Development Projects Among East African Pastoralists." *African Studies Review,* 21 (1978): 49-63.

Grezenbach, K. "Structural Change in the Location of Agriculture as a Result of Increased Density of Population in Densely Populated Fringe Regions of the Humid African Tropics: Examples from S. Senegal and N. Tanzania." Giessen, West Germany: Geographisches Institut, Universität Giessen, *Reihe,* 3 (1977): 13-14.

Gulbrandsen, O. *Agro-Pastoral Production and Communal Land Use.* Gaberone, Botswana: Government Printer, 1980.

Harwitz, M. "On Improving the Lot of the Poorest: Economic Plans in Kenya." *African Studies Review,* 21 (1978): 65-73.

International Labour Office. *Employment, Incomes and Equality: A Strategy for Increasing Productive Employment in Kenya.* Geneva: ILO, 1972.

Johnson, S. L. "Changing Patterns of Maize Utilization in Kenya." *Studies in Third World Societies,* 8 (1979): 37-56.

Johnson, W. "Towards a Food and Nutrition Policy in Tanzania." *Food Policy,* 5 (1980): 143-147.

Kabweayere, T. B. "Land and the Growth of Social Stratification in Uganda." *Journal of Eastern African Research and Development*, 5 (1975): 1–17.

King, R. *Land Reform, A World Survey.* London: G. Bell and Sons, Ltd., 1977.

Kjaerby, F. *Problems and Contradictions in the Development of Ox-Cultivation in Tanzania.* Copenhagen: Scandinavian Institute of African Studies, 1983.

Leys, C. "Development Strategy in Kenya Since 1971." *Journal of African Studies*, 13 (1979): 295–320.

Luttrell, W. L. "Locational Planning and Regional Development in Tanzania." *Development and Change*, 4 (1972): 17–38.

Mascarenhas, A. C. *Food Production, The Total Environment, and Rural Development.* Dar es Salaam: Bureau of Resource Assessment and Land Use Planning, University of Dar es Salaam, 1977.

Mbithi, P. M. and C. Barnes. *The Spontaneous Settlement Problem in Kenya.* Nairobi: East African Literature Bureau, 1975.

McKelvy, J. *Man Against Tsetse: Struggle for Africa.* Ithaca: Cornell University Press, 1973.

Mergen, F. et al. *Status of Conditions in Tropical Forests.* New Haven, CN: Yale University School of Forestry and Environmental Studies, 1981.

Monod, T. *Pastoralism in Tropical Africa.* London: Oxford University Press, 1975.

Moore, J. E. *Rural Population Carrying Capabilities for the Districts of Tanzania.* Dar es Salaam: Bureau of Resource Assessment and Land Use Planning, University of Dar es Salaam, 1971.

Moran, E. F. et al. "Changing Agricultural Systems in Africa." *Studies in Third World Societies*, 8 (1979): 1–138.

Muiruri, W. "Bio-Economic Conflicts in Resource Use and Management: A Kenyan Case Study." *Geo-Journal*, 2 (1978): 321–330.

Odegi-Awvondo, C. "Wildlife Conservation and the Decline of Pastoralism in Kenya," *African Journal of Sociology*, 2 (1982): 74–83.

Odinga, R. S. *The Kenya Highlands: Land Use and Agricultural Development.* Nairobi: East African Publishing House, 1979.

Pevetz, W. *African Agrarian Problems.* Vienna: Agrarwirtschaftlichen Instituts des Bundesministeriums für Land und Fortwirtschaft, 1975.

Putterman, L. "A Modified Collective Agriculture in Rural Growth-With-Equity: Reconsidering the Private Unimodal Solution." *World Development*, 11 (1983): 77–100.

Qvortrup, S. A. and L. H. Blackenship. "Vegetation of Kekopey: A Kenya Cattle Ranch." *East African Agricultural and Forestry Journal*, 40 (1975): 439–447.

Rald, J. and K. Rald. *Rural Organization in Bukoba District, Tanzania.* Uppsala, Sweden: Scandinavian Institute of African Studies, 1975.

Richards, P. "Ecological Change and the Politics of African Land Use." *African Studies Review*, 26 (1983): 1–72.

Ruthenberg, H. "Outline of a Strategy for Agricultural Development in Kenya."

Quarterly Journal of International Agriculture, 19 (1980): 6–17.

Schneider, H. K. "Economic Development and Economic Change: The Case of East African Cattle." *Current Anthropology,* 15 (1974): 259–279.

Simpson, M. C. "Alternative Strategies for Rangeland Development in Kenya." *Rural Development Study No. 2.* Leeds, U.K.: Unviersity of Leeds, March 1973.

Stoces, F. "Place of Agriculture in the East African Economy, 1955–1963." *Agricultural Economics Bulletin for Africa,* 9 (1962): 79–104.

Thimm, H. U. "Back to the Land: Aspects of Land Use Policy in Kenya." *Eastern African Journal of Rural Development,* 6 (1973): 157–164.

Thomas, I. D. *Some Notes on Population and Land Use in the North Pare Mountains.* Dar es Salaam: Bureau of Resource Assessment and Land Use Planning, University of Dar es Salaam, 1970.

Thresher, P. "The Economics of Domesticated Oryx Compared with That of Cattle." *World Animal Review,* 36 (1980): 37–43.

Tschanneri, G. "Rural Water Supply in Tanzania: Is 'Politics' or 'Technique' in Command?" *African Review,* 6 (1976): 108–166.

Index

Italicized page numbers refer to figures and tables.